the **meditation** year

the **meditation** year

jane**hope**

STOREY
BOOKS

The mission of Storey Publishing is to serve our customers by publishing practical information that encourages personal independence in harmony with the environment.

United States edition published in 2001 by Storey Books,
210 MASS MoCA Way, North Adams, MA 01247

United Kingdom edition published in 2001 by MQ Publications Ltd,
12 The Ivories, 6–8 Northampton Street, London N1 2HY

Editor: Kate John, MQ Publications Ltd; Janet Lape, Storey Publishing
Editorial Director: Ljiljana Baird, MQ Publications Ltd; Deborah Balmuth, Storey Publishing
Art Direction: John Casey, MQ Publications Ltd; Meredith Maker, Storey Publishing
Illustrators: Penny Brown and Jane Hope

The information in this book is true and complete to the best of our knowledge. All recommendations are made without guarantee on the part of the author or Storey Books. The author and publisher disclaim any liability in connection with the use of this information. For additional information please contact Storey Books, 210 MASS MoCA Way, North Adams, MA 01247.

Printed in China

Library of Congress Cataloging-in-Publication Data

Hope, Jane
The meditation year : a seasonal guide to contemplation, relaxation, and visualization / by Jane Hope.
p. cm.
ISBN 1-58017-427-2 (alk. Paper)
1. Meditation. I. Title.

BL627 .H64 2001
291.4'35—dc21

2001041135

contents

introduction

Everyone in the world wants to find peace of mind and avoid suffering or unhappiness. Delight or misery are, to a large extent, dependent upon our state of mind. Meditation works with the mind itself and allows us to take responsibility for positive change. It teaches us how to use the mind's potential to meet the challenges that our lives present.

The word meditation has many meanings but its ancient roots go back to Sanskrit words related to healing, wisdom, and learning. Throughout history, the world's religious traditions have made use of a vast number of meditative disciplines. There are many ways to meditate but a common theme runs though all the different methods. Each is concerned with bringing the mind back from the teeming, noisy chaos of thoughts and emotions to quietness and silence—the still point of the turning world. All of the different kinds of meditation seek to free the mind from its egocentric concerns and to teach it to dwell in the present moment.

In a traditional Hindu text, the mind is likened to the surface of a lake ruffled by the wind. When the wind blows, the waves break up and their reflections can only be seen in fragmented form. In calm weather, the reflections of sky and clouds become translucently vivid and one can see into the very depths of the crystal clear water. The practice of meditation causes the winds of distraction to subside and allow the waters of the mind to return to their original clarity and stillness. It is only through regular and steady practice that you can see any of the benefits of meditation; they cannot be accomplished overnight. If you are patient, however, you will begin to see positive changes.

Meditation relaxes the body, brings clarity and steadiness of mind, and opens the heart. It allows you to see your life in a new perspective and brings a greater sense of delight and spontaneity to your days. This book is a guide to the start of an exciting journey of self-discovery.

how to use this book

Many people today are interested in learning to meditate but do not want to become involved in any religion or faith. In the past, meditation practices were almost exclusively found within the great religious or contemplative traditions but today it is possible to learn to meditate without becoming part of any particular faith. Many of the meditation techniques in this book come from the Buddhist tradition, but they do not require any belief or affiliation and can be practiced by anyone.

Learning any new skill takes time but by simply following the instructions given in this book, you will learn meditation easily and experience the benefits quickly. All of the meditations in this book are safe and easy to practice. The meditations are divided into four main sections, each representing a seasonal quarter of the year. The first section, "Awakening," provides an essential foundation on which to build your meditation practice. Take your time to learn these techniques: They will steady your body and mind, giving you the stability to try other practices. Some techniques will feel more comfortable than others; this is perfectly normal but persevere a little with the practices that feel less smooth. Most importantly, go slowly and adopt new methods only when you feel ready.

In the second section, "Opening," learn the simple act of turning yourself toward new experiences and how to enjoy a new depth of acceptance and understanding. Meditations include concentrating the mind on walking, and how to focus on the task itself rather than the goal—bringing your awareness into the present moment. This section also explains how relaxation plays an important role in helping to acknowledge personal tension and stress, and how to "let go."

In "Fruition," the third section in this book, discover the great fulfillment of expressing loving kindness to yourself, and to those around you. Being aware of your sense perceptions is a valuable way to see everything more clearly, while the use of mantra in meditation helps to steady the mind, keeping it from wandering into its usual turbulent wave of thoughts.

Finally, the fourth section, "Transformation," introduces the practice of concentration through visualization—a positive workout for the mind—to help you achieve mental clarity. This is a valuable exercise in improving personal concentration during each meditation you practice. Learn about the benefits of going on retreat, and the different ways in which you can find a meditation teacher to work with.

a time to practice

Once you have made the decision to begin meditation, you need to take practical steps to include it as a natural part of your daily life. As with any new activity you learn, it is good to make practice a regular habit, so that you find you can do it even when you feel down or discouraged. It is particularly valuable to be able to meditate during the low times as well as when you are feeling inspired and cheerful.

❶ If you have a busy schedule, it is often hard to find time for meditation. There are always pressing commitments to fulfill. Keep reminding yourself that you would feel less pressured if you put aside just a short time each day for your meditation.

❷ Choose a time of day for practice that is suitable for you. A morning person may have no difficulty in fitting in half an hour before work, whereas night owls can find evening meditation more relaxing and restorative. Either time is fine.

❸ At first, meditate only for a short time, maybe for ten minutes, and end the session while your body and mind are still fresh. Meditation should not become a burden: If you push yourself too much at the beginning, you will lose your enthusiasm.

❹ Decide on the length of time you want to meditate and stick to it, even if the practice seems to be going well. As you become more experienced, you can increase the length of the sessions.

❺ Regular daily meditation is the most effective way to practice. However, if you find that long gaps occur between your meditations, don't be discouraged. Now is a good time to start again—with meditation you can always make a fresh start.

a place to practice

❶ Reserve a place especially for your meditation sessions. Try to keep it free from clutter, and, if possible, place reminders of other projects such as work, hobbies, or reading out of sight: They may distract.

❷ Keep your meditation space quiet and clean; make it a place you feel glad to be in and where, ideally, you cannot be disturbed.

❸ Set up your seat on a cushion on the floor, or on the bed. If you use a chair, ensure you can sit comfortably on it without leaning back.

❹ Light a candle and some incense at the beginning of the session. Many people find this small ritual a powerful way of focusing the mind at the beginning, and use the putting out of the lights as a satisfying way to end.

❺ Lastly, switch off your mobile phone and let the voice-mail take the calls. This is time for yourself.

spring

awakening

Spring is the time of awakening. After the cold of winter, new life starts to stir and the world wakes up again. There is a sense of anticipation in the air and a feeling that all things are possible.

Starting to meditate brings the same feeling of hopefulness and awakening. It allows us to be fully present in the wakefulness of each moment of nowness. Experience becomes fresh and vivid. The mind has space to relax and expand. In that awake, relaxed state, we become aware of our thoughts, our feelings and our body. It is like waking from a long sleep.

month 1

month 2

month 3

month 1

Meditation begins with the body. We learn to sit like a mountain: Steadfast, enduring, and majestic.

contents:

body and mind

The first month of the year is a time of renewal; it's a time to look back at the successes and failures of the past year, and make new resolutions to change life for the better. For many people, the fast-pace and frenzy of modern living leads to a feeling of being stressed and burnt out and a constant sense of not being able to enjoy the present moment.

The first meditation of the year teaches how to synchronize body and mind. When your mind and body are unsynchronized, the mind can speed ahead of the body. You lose things, forget what you are doing, and don't really connect with what's around you. When you bring mind and body together, the speed and confusion melt away, enabling you to appreciate the details of your world and, suddenly, you have enough time to do things completely.

Being aware of the body is important. Western culture has, in the past, viewed the body as inferior to the mind and spirit, the purpose of Western Christian spirituality being to transcend the material world. In many Eastern traditions, however, the body is honored as sacred. As Westerners, when we begin meditation, we often think the posture of the body is unimportant, "real" meditation being all about the mind. But actually, the physical posture adopted affects the mind in a fundamental way.

Mind and body are intimately connected. When you are at ease and contented, the body has no sense of tension, and you feel relaxed and expansive. When you are anxious and worried, the body automatically tenses up: You hunch your shoulders and begin to slouch. Bad news automatically brings tension and contraction; good news automatically brings relaxation and expansion.

When you begin meditation, however, you might feel that your body is a problem. You could experience a surprising amount of physical pain, and this pain is only partly caused by sitting in an unfamiliar position. Working with the body requires gentleness and patience because old pain and tension have become locked into its structure and cannot dissolve quickly. During meditation you quickly become aware of all of the tension in your back, shoulders, jaw, and other places that has gradually accumulated in the past. The experience of this pain, far from being a negative thing, is an important sign that you are beginning to release all that locked-in tension that has built up over the years.

It is important to realize that meditation is not concerned with trying to get away from where you are. Relating to your body is one of the most valuable lessons to be learned. Many people feel aggression toward their bodies: In meditation, you will begin to know and accept the needs of your body in a new and loving way.

sitting like a mountain

One of the definitions of meditation is having a steady mind, and the aim of meditation is not to identify so closely with thoughts but rather, just to watch them come and go. In daily life, you usually react to what is happening in the mind. When you feel happy, you call a friend or write a poem; when you're feeling down, you might pour a drink or turn on the television. The discipline of meditation allows you to sit like a mountain with all kinds of weather passing overhead—storms, sun, wind, rain. Nothing that is thrown up causes a great reaction; you are just aware of the passing weather. The mountain remains firm and solid and steady, not rocked by the changes that happen all around. Meditation allows everyone to develop such firmness and dignity.

taking your seat

There is a clear connection between the body's posture during meditation and the attitude of the mind. When the body is upright and relaxed, it is easy for the meditation to take place naturally, for the way you sit reflects the essential nature of your being: Wakeful, open, and responsive *(see pages 18–19)*.

In the West, we tend to be fascinated by technique, but as long as you are comfortable, your sitting technique is not the most important aspect of meditation. What's important is your intention, and your willingness to to be open to experience.

In meditation you are not working on the mind alone. When you sit in meditation, you bring mind and body together. Meditation is a very basic, simple activity, but because it is so simple and basic, it often seems difficult—it is so different from the complicated busyness of regular living. When you sit quietly, the body begins to settle and rest. At first, the mind, unaccustomed to the sense of repose, frantically tries to find entertainment, but wait, and it begins to settle and rest too.

establishing the posture

Meditation is not a method of running away from the world or escaping into a trancelike state. It is a direct way to relate to the world and to your experience of it. The very posture you adopt embodies a wakefulness and gentleness that allows you to do this.

1 First find a comfortable place to sit. If you are not used to sitting on the floor, use a chair. If you prefer, sit on a cushion or stool, at least eight inches (20cm) high off the ground. (Feel free to improvise: Two telephone directories, covered by a cushion, is ideal).

2 Sit (cross-legged on the floor, cushion, or stool) with your back straight and upright, your shoulders open and relaxed, and your hands resting comfortably with your palms on your knees or thighs. Adjust the posture until you feel stable and "planted." Most importantly, keep the spine relaxed and upright, as if the vertebrae were a pile of coins. When your back is straight, "inner energy" can flow through your body.

3 Keep your shoulders open, with a feeling that your heart is exposed. Feel great strength in your back and a gentleness in your front and chest area.

4 Let your mouth open slightly, as if saying "aaaah," to relax any tension in the jaw.

5 Keep your eyes open, looking downward at an angle of about 45 degrees in front. Do not focus on anything in particular; just let your gaze expand and become more spacious. With the eyes open, you are less likely to fall asleep—meditation is not a trancelike state.

benefits of this month's meditation

- Better posture
- Physical relaxation
- Increased ability to enjoy the present moment
- Greater awareness of the body
- Reduced impulsive reactions to emotions and thoughts

meditation 1—equanimity

Often we feel unsettled by our thoughts, knocked off balance by their force and urgency, but when we practice this meditation we learn to return to the present moment of nowness again and again. In this way, we begin to trust that the present moment contains all we need, and we become less attached to our feelings, fears, and solid ideas of what we are and what the world is. In this way, we develop equanimity and learn to dance with changing circumstances rather than fight them.

❶ Sit, as if you were on a throne, with dignity and stability. Allow your breath to move gently through your body. Let each breath be like a sigh, bringing with it a wave of calmness and relaxation.

❷ Become aware of what feels closed and constricted in your body, your mind, and your heart. With each breath, let space open up those closed-in feelings. Let your mind expand into space, unobstructed and relaxed. Open your mind, your emotions, and your senses. Note whatever feelings, images, emotions, or sensations come to you.

❸ Each time you feel carried away on a wave of thought, return to your sense of steadiness and connection with the earth. Feel as if you were sitting on a throne in the very heart of your world. As you sit, appreciate moments of stability and peace in life. Reflect on how the feelings, emotions, and stories that appear in your mind come into existence and then disappear. Return to your body and rest for a moment in the equanimity and peace that exists in the center of your thoughts, dreams, and memories.

❹ Sit, in this way, for 10 minutes, then slowly stand up and take a few steps, walking with the same sense of awareness. Watch how your sense of solidity and balance continues after the meditation is over.

flight from the shadow

"Flight from the shadow" is a story by Chuang Tzu, a third-century B.C.E. Chinese sage of the Taoist tradition. Many of Chuang Tzu's stories are extremely funny but, at the same time, point out profound insights into the human condition. The following tale is just such an example.

"Once there was a man who was so troubled by the sight of his own shadow and so disturbed by his footsteps that he decided to get rid of both. His method of escape was to run away from them, so he got up and ran. But each time he put his foot down, there was another step, and his shadow had no difficulty at all in keeping up. He blamed his failure on not running away fast enough. So he ran quicker and quicker until finally he dropped dead. The man did not realize that if only he found some shade, his shadow would vanish, and that if he sat down quietly, there would be no footsteps."

This story illustrates with great humor the fact that all our strategies for finding peace by running away from things do not work. Meditation means finding that quiet, shady place where we no longer run away from shadows or footsteps. Peace can only be attained by "taking the one seat."

questions and answers

question

Usually I have no problems sitting cross-legged, but recently I seem to be experiencing more pain than when I started meditating. Why might this be?

answer

It often happens that, after you have been meditating for a while and have become accustomed to the posture, restlessness starts to manifest as physical pain. Instead of trying to adjust to a more comfortable position immediately, it's useful to look at and feel the quality of the pain. Often you will find that this kind of pain dies away of its own accord. If it does not, change position!

Much physical discomfort is mind-related and arises from unresolved and deep-seated fears, anxieties, or anger. A simple way to help ease this kind of pain or tension is to breathe deeply and slowly into the pain, and then imagine the tension easing out of the body. In future months, we will learn ways of meditating that help with these unresolved issues.

question
I felt quite a lot of pain in my body when I meditated. What can I do about this?

answer
Meditation flows more smoothly if you are physically relaxed. As a beginner to meditation, your body may be unaccustomed to sitting upright. Do not push yourself too hard, and keep the meditation short at first. Experiment with small shifts in posture: Try tilting your pelvis forward a little, or shifting from side to side. You could ask someone to tell you whether your back is straight: Leaning to one side may be creating a lot of tension. Don't try to sit in one position for too long but, rather, sit with your knees up for a while or sit on a chair for part of the time you meditate. Meditation should not feel like a test of endurance.

daily meditation reminders

Meditation is not something to perform only at a special time and in a particular place. After you have practiced the first formal meditation on pages 22–23 a few times, try using the following brief reminders throughout the day. But keep these mini meditations very short—don't practice for more than a minute at a time.

1 Check your posture throughout the day: Notice how you sit habitually, then relax, straighten your spine, and open up your shoulders. Breathe deeply from your lower abdomen.

2 When you notice tension in your body, let your awareness rest on where the tension is, then let your breath spread through the body, loosening those tight, constricted feelings.

3 Place a postcard of a mountain somewhere where you'll see it frequently—perhaps on the refrigerator, or above your desk at work. Use it as a reminder to reconnect with the image. Feel the solidity and unperturbable quality of the mountain. Again, breathe deeply from your lower abdomen.

thoughts for the month

When doing formal meditation practice, you give yourself time to feel exactly what is happening in the body. The daily meditation reminders allow you to bring that awareness into all regular daily activities. This is important in that it teaches first ways to understand how you hold tension and hurt in the bodies, and then how to let go. Staying grounded in the experience of the body is essential to the development of balance and equanimity.

After a while, meditation becomes an essential part of life, as regular an activity as brushing your teeth or washing your face. If you practice meditation regularly, you will find that life starts to feel more spacious, you feel less hassled by events or people, and you begin to live more in the present moment, your mind less ambushed by anxiety about the future or regrets about the past.

meditation in the buddhist tradition

The process of meditation is the cornerstone of Buddhist tradition. Sakyamuni Buddha, founder of the Buddhist religion, was an ordinary man with no claims to divine origin—the name "Buddha" simply means "one who is awake," and he taught that the way to become awake or enlightened is through practicing meditation.

The Buddhist tradition is transmitted directly through personal experience of meditation, and not through beliefs or doctrine. It relies on people experiencing the truth for themselves.

The Buddha's principle teaching was of the Four Noble Truths. His first statement was that human beings experience suffering because of distorted beliefs about the nature of reality. He said that suffering begins from basic bewilderment. From that fundamental state of bewilderment, we base our perceptions on an idea of ego as a permanent entity. We seek to find permanence and security where they are not available, and the more we try to do this, the more painful and unsatisfying life becomes.

Buddhism recognizes that all human beings experience glimpses of enlightenment when the ego does not interfere with moments of total direct experience. These glimpses of enlightenment motivate people to find a way out of confusion and discontent. The Buddha taught that ordinary people can become enlightened and that the path to liberation and freedom comes through the practice of meditation. Many people believe that the Buddha's teachings are pessimistic because of their emphasis on suffering, but representations of the Buddha always portray a radiant, serene appearance that derives from an acceptance of things as they are.

The original form of Buddhism in India died out around the 13th century, but, by that time, many different schools had become established throughout Asia, Tibet, China, Korea, and Japan.

In southeast Asia, the form of Buddhism stayed close to the original teachings of the Buddha. The monastic life is accepted as the ideal way to reach liberation, and the lay population supports monks and nuns. This form of Buddhism is still alive in Thailand, Burma, and other parts of Asia.

One of the most distinctive forms of Buddhism is Zen, the

form that developed in Japan. The term Zen derives from a Sanskrit word for meditation, and meditation occupies a central position in Zen practice. The essence of Zen meditation is to remain entirely focused on the present moment. The immediacy and spontaneity of Zen Buddhism influenced all of the arts in Japan, and led to new ways of practicing various other disciplines, such as writing poetry, flower arranging, martial arts, and even drinking tea.

Another distinctive form of Buddhism is practiced in Tibet and the Himalayan regions and is known as Vajrayana or Tantra. The unique quality of Vajrayana is that it brings the precise experience of the awakened state into everyday life. The monastic ideal is not held to be as important as in other forms of Buddhism, and the essence of Vajrayana is that any circumstances can be used as a way to develop wakefulness. The tradition has stories of people from all walks of life who became enlightened through meditative practice.

Buddhism is now the fastest growing belief system in the West, where it is beginning to develop its own shape, with an emphasis on community rather than the monastic life. The heart of the teaching remains the same, based on simple meditation.

month2

Our breath is the bridge from our body to our mind.
Joining body and mind by the breath brings deep
inner healing.

contents:

coming home to yourself

After the excitement of the new year's beginning, it's common to experience a sense of anticlimax. Some days, we feel empty, tired, and joyless—not really our true selves at all. At times like these, even trying to be cheerful makes no difference, and it's easy to feel there's nothing left to give. When body and mind are low and dispirited, meditation can help heal physically and emotionally. So, on those days when nothing seems to go right, simply close the door on the outside world and use the opportunity to come back to your true self with meditation.

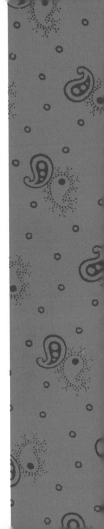

the foundation of practice

Over weeks of use, this month's meditation begins to feel very natural, and yet some cycles will still seem more difficult than others. One day, the meditation is calm and joyful; the next day, the mind is a whirlpool of thoughts and distractions. This is quite natural; keep in mind the notion of "sitting like a mountain" *(see page 18)*, and regard the storms and clear days merely as the changing patterns of your own mental weather system.

healing body and mind through meditation

In meditation, we become aware of the body and mind in a new way. This is helpful in a culture that has neglected the physical, intuitive, and emotional world in favor of the rational and intellectual. Often the pain encountered in meditation is a physical manifestation of emotional and spiritual blocks locked into the body by muscles that have tightened over the years. Meditation begins to bring loving attention to these physical blocks, and to feelings locked away over a lifetime, and allows us to start to work with them again.

breathing—the essence of balance

The breath is the bridge from the body to the mind. It is the one constant element in life and can reconcile mind and body, bringing about very profound reintegration and healing.

All of the ancient languages use the same words for breath as for soul or spirit. In Latin *spirare* means "to breathe," and *spiritus* means "spirit." The root of both words is found in the term "inspiration," which literally means "in-breathing," and so is, in essence, linked with breathing in. In the Biblical tradition, it is said that God breathed divine life into the earth that he made, and in this way the first human being was formed. In Hindi, a person with great spiritual attainment is called *mahatma;* which means both "great soul" and "great breath." Also in Indian teachings, the breath is considered the bearer of each person's lifeforce, known as *prana.*

Breathing is a constant rhythmic activity with two phases: Inspiration and expiration. We could describe the two poles of breathing in terms of relaxation and tension. In panic attacks or when we are very anxious, we breathe in so much that we hyperventilate. Balance can then be achieved only by losing consciousness, at which point normal breathing starts again spontaneously.

In total relaxation, when the body feels completely loose and free, there is no constriction or tightness and the breath becomes deep and full. When we are tense, we breathe from the top of the lungs; but when we relax, all of the air is expelled from the very bottom of the lungs.

In meditation we do not manipulate the breath by forcing it into a deeper rhythm, but, by allowing mind and body to find its own repose, the breath alters and deepens spontaneously.

When tense or afraid or angry, we tend to breathe in and hold the breath. When things get too much, we say "it takes our breath away," and when we feel restricted and claustrophobic, we state that we "can't catch our breath."

On the other hand, when we are relaxed or happy or at ease, we tend to sigh and breathe out, and this, too, is reflected in language. After a release of tension, we say that we can "breathe freely" again. In the constant alternation between holding on and letting go, breathing allows body and mind to relax and release.

benefits of this month's meditation

- Increased "breathing space"
- Equanimity
- Less attachment to the solidity of your thoughts
- Calmer patterns of breathing

meditation 2—using the breath as a focus

This month's meditation begins to use the breath as a focus for attention.

1 Start by sitting on a cushion or stool, or on a chair *(see pages 20–21)*, legs crossed, back straight and upright, shoulders relaxed and open, palms on the knees or thighs, mouth slightly open, eyes open and gaze down.

2 Focus by remembering why you want to meditate. Reflect on your need for peace of mind. Recall the tension in your body and affirm that you want to release that stress. Encourage yourself.

3 Let your body relax. Ease into the posture by shifting from side to side a little until you feel "planted." Briefly touch into the feelings in your body, and consciously soften any obvious tension or tightness. Let go of surface thoughts or plans.

meditation 2—using the breath as a focus

4 Rest your attention lightly on your breathing. At first, just be aware of the breath naturally coming in and going out of your body. You do not need to change the breath in any way; just be aware of it. Don't force the breath into a different rhythm.

5 Feel the sensations of your natural breathing carefully, relaxing into each breath as you feel it, and noticing how the sensation of breathing changes with the in-breath and the out-breath.

6 Focus your attention more closely on the out-breath. Rather than watching the breath, let yourself be with the breath, become the breath. Let the breath, the breather, and the breathing become one. Breathing is panoramic: Experience the breath as an expansion from the whole body. At the end of the out-breath, let it go into the space of the room around you.

❼ Just let the in-breath come; you need not focus on it at all. If, however, you find that your awareness carries on through both in-breath and out-breath, this is fine.

❽ After a while, you will notice that you were thinking about something. Maybe about the meditation itself, but your mind was wandering. At this point, simply bring yourself back to the breath. Before you return, acknowledge that you have been wandering by saying gently to yourself, "thinking," or "wandering." Make the acknowledgment very gently but firmly. In this way, the mind disengages from thoughts and returns to the breath.

❾ At the end of the meditation session, while still seated, reflect briefly on your experience. Then gradually get up. Do not immediately engage in activity—allow time to experience the sense of relaxation.This month's meditation begins to use the breath as a focus for attention.

questions and answers

question
No matter how hard I try, I can't seem to rid myself of thoughts. What can I do?

answer
When you meditate, you become more aware of your thought process—and that's an important part of meditation. If you make thoughts into the enemy, you will find them more and more disturbing. The trick is not to try too hard to rid yourself of thoughts; rather, just see them for what they are. Whether your thoughts are crazy and emotional, or light and ephemeral, keep your reaction the same. Just notice them and return to the breathing. You don't have to get rid of your thoughts; they are a natural process.

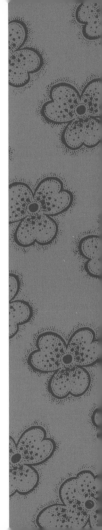

question

Some thoughts in meditation seem really important; I get frustrated that I can't do something about them. What can I do about this?

answer

When you meditate, your mind becomes less frenetic, and often you do become aware of important issues in life. Make a mental note to remember those issues after the meditation session. However, you may find that those insistent thoughts are not so urgent. When you disengage from them and come back to the breath, you become less ruled by their power and importance.

daily meditation reminders

Remember to keep these brief reminder meditations very short—no longer than a minute at a time.

❶ Check back to the experience of breathing. Let your mind return to your body and your breath. Tune into the natural rhythm of your breath.

❷ Watch your breathing patterns; notice whether your breathing is shallow and rapid, or deep and slow. Do not attempt to change the patterns but see if you can note what makes your breathing change.

❸ When you are angry, watch what happens to your pattern of breathing.

❹ Look at your thought patterns—are you anxious, relaxed, jealous, restless, tender, or fearful? Gently examine what's going on in your mind without exercising any sense of judgement. Do not try to push your thoughts away—just touch base and let go.

thoughts for the month

A simple technique, the meditation on the breath is essential as your main practice and an excellent basis for the meditations to come in future months. Once you become familiar with the technique and have achieved some stability in your posture, it is time to try other techniques. The breathing meditation provides a safe and trustworthy foundation to build on, and the practice is one to come back to naturally. Without this stable foundation, you risk merely changing from one method to another, and not gaining genuine experience from any of the methods you try.

meditation in the hindu tradition

The earliest traces of human civilization were found in the Indus valley and date back to around 3000 B.C.E. From the very beginning of Indian civilization, there is evidence that yoga and meditation were practiced. Archeological finds identify an ancient image of a yogi sitting cross-legged in the lotus position as Shiva, an important figure in later Indian religion. The earliest sacred scriptures in the world, the Vedas, date from before 1200 B.C.E. The word Veda means "knowledge," and our own word "wisdom" derives from the same ancient root.

Classical Hinduism offers many different ways for human beings to achieve liberation, or release from the perpetual cycle of reincarnation. Hatha yoga, with its regime of physical postures and breathing exercises, is the system that has become most widely known outside India. It involves a meditation technique for calming and focusing the mind. A vow to practice non-violence (ahimsa) may also be taken, and this often involves becoming vegetarian and not killing animals for food.

The word "yoga" derives from the verb "to yoke," implying yoking the body to the mind and also the soul to God.

There are many forms of yoga, including: karma yoga (the pursuit of action devoted to God), jnana yoga (the path of wisdom), bhakti yoga (devotion to the guru), and raja, royal, or classical, yoga (a path that combines many ways).

Hinduism recognizes four stages in a person's religious life. The first is childhood; the second, study; and the third is the life of a householder, busy with the world of work, marriage, and raising a family. The fourth and final stage involves leaving behind worldly concerns and becoming a "forest dweller," as a wandering ascetic. In the fourth stage of life, a person forgoes home and family to concentrate on the spiritual side of life. Forest dwellers often shave their heads and wear orange robes to signify their renunciation of the world; the community rewards them with support and alms.

The scope of Hinduism's spiritual practices is vast; meditation, ritual, and devotion are sewn into the fabric of Indian culture. All the paths, however, seek to transcend duality and seek union with the divine.

It is important to cross the "boredom threshold" with your meditation practice and if you constantly try new methods, you will never go through this important stage.

When you meditate, you do not allow your mind to follow any of its normal patterns. Deprived of the familiarity of those habitual thoughts, the mind experiences some discomfort. Boredom is the name we give to that edgy, slightly uncomfortable feeling.

If we persevere further, however, that discomfort starts to recede, and we begin to trust the relative emptiness of the present moment. Experiencing that barrier of discomfort is a very important stage in meditation. We can only cross that barrier with a meditation technique which has become very ordinary and everyday.

To transcend duality, the seeker must enter a state in which the person experiencing and the object merge. This state is called "samadhi," and it is the goal of all the different paths in Hinduism. Hindu belief teaches that the mind is filled with thought waves, and that we usually experience these turbulent waves as reality. However, by stilling the mind in meditation, these thought waves subside, and reality is seen to be as vast as the ocean. When the mind is clear and still, it is possible to experience the true reality of cosmic consciousness, union with God.

month3

By coming back to the center, we return from the exterior to the interior, from time to timelessness and from diversity to oneness.

contents:

becoming centered

When fresh possibilities present themselves, we make plans and look forward to new ventures. Life seems very exciting and full of new promise, but particularly at times like these, it is important to guard against becoming too scattered and restless.

At such times, the mind can be like a wild monkey, jumping from one thought to the next, and it is all too easy to become involved in a multitude of distracting activities. In constantly seeking happiness in the outer world, we become increasingly busy, trying to achieve satisfaction. Yet, satisfaction is always out of reach, so we spin faster and faster in the search, forgetting that the only true way of achieving peace is to return to the center of our being. By coming back to the center, we return from exterior to interior, from time to timelessness, and from diversity to oneness. Learning how to become centered extends to every part of life, like a ripple spreading in still water.

centering

One of most basic meditation techniques, centering develops an ability to be focused and calm. It is the practice of holding continuous awareness of an object or sensation, while at the same time being completely wakeful and aware of the environment around you. The center is the object or sensation you are using as a focus.

Centering develops steadiness of mind, too. When your mind is centered, it is like a securely anchored boat. Although the boat might drift back and forth, it does not get washed away in the current. Each time it drifts too far, the anchor chain tightens, and the boat is brought back again and again to the fixed point. Similarly, in meditation, the mind naturally drifts back and forth, but the focus of the meditation is the anchor chain that keeps bringing you back.

benefits of this month's meditation

- Steadiness of mind
- Improved focus of awareness
- Increased attention span
- Improved ability to ignore distractions

meditation 3—
centering on the hara

The focus for this meditation is maintaining awareness of the sensations in your lower abdomen, about two inches (5cm) below the navel. This is the *tantien* or *hara*—the center of gravity of your physical body. It is a very useful technique when your mind feels scattered or overexcited.

❶ Loosen tight clothing. Sit in a comfortable, relaxed way *(see pages 20-21)*.

❷ Focus on why you want to become centered and the intention of maintaining your awareness on the hara.

❸ At first you may want to focus your attention more clearly by placing your hands on your abdomen. Rest your thumbs just above your navel, palms facing in.

❹ When your awareness is focused on the hara, rest your hands on your knees. If you lose the sensation of the lower abdomen at any time, place your hands back there.

❺ Breathe naturally, observing the slight rise and fall of the abdomen as you breathe in and out.

❻ Do not become so absorbed in the sensation of the hara that you lose awareness of the environment. Your awareness will naturally shift between the environment and the hara. Like the analogy of the boat at anchor, let your awareness be anchored by the hara, but not fixed so firmly that your mind cannot move a little.

❼ When you find yourself thinking, disengage from the thoughts. Do not suppress your thoughts, merely recognize that they are inappropriate at this time.

❽ Don't worry about how long you can concentrate, but on how often you disengage from your thoughts and return to your focus. When you can focus your attention on the hara for about 30 seconds without distraction, you are ready to move on.

questions and answers

question
The moment I sit down to meditate I fall asleep.
This happens even though I am not tired. Can I do anything about this?

answer
This is the most common problem for people with hectic, busy lives. Sleepiness during meditation has several causes. Often it is simply due to physical tiredness. Acknowledge this kind of tiredness as a signal to respect the needs of the body more, and rest. It's not usually a problem thereafter.

There are several small ways in which you can try to remedy a feeling of drowsiness. The first is to change your posture by sitting up straighter. The next is to raise your gaze for a while so you are looking forward rather than down. You could also try opening a window or splashing your face with water. However, if nothing else seems to work, there is nothing wrong with taking a nap. Often, if you allow yourself to fall asleep, you will suddenly wake up and feel wide awake again.

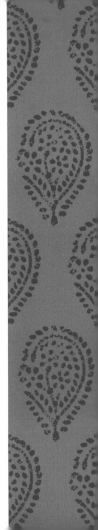

During meditation, we sometimes encounter some aspect of life we have been trying to avoid or not paying attention to. In the deep relaxation of meditation, old pain often surfaces, bringing us head to head with feelings of sorrow, anger, or loneliness. In an effort to avoid giving attention to these rejected emotions, it is often easier to fall asleep. So, if you find yourself falling asleep in meditation, even though you are not tired, if might be good to ask yourself whether there is something you are trying to avoid. When we recognize the resistance to seeing emotional blockages, meditation practice becomes a great opportunity for self discovery.

daily meditation reminders

Meditation is not something to practice only in a formal setting. Learning to focus quickly in all kinds of situations is a valuable way of staying flexible and calm. Here are step-by-step instructions for centering yourself quickly. Practice them whenever and wherever you need them during the day—traveling on the subway, standing in line in a store, before falling asleep, during TV advertisements, or during quiet times at work.

1 When you become aware that your thoughts are chaotic and speedy, bring your mind quickly back to the hara *(see pages 56–57)*.

2 Let your awareness rest on the hara for a few seconds, and take a deep breath.

3 Stop practicing after bringing your mind back to the hara several times. Don't repeat for more than a minute each time—you are simply training your mind to respond flexibly and quickly.

thoughts for the month

For many people today, leading a quiet, contemplative existence is not an option. The pace of life grows faster and faster, making relaxation seem totally out of reach. However, meditation techniques allow you to harmonize your body, mind, and spirit. This in turn enables you to fulfill all your responsibilities and commitments while at the same time finding peace in the middle of activity.

It would be unrealistic to expect meditation to be an answer to all of our problems. There is no magic that will suddenly change everything in your life.

What meditation gives you, however, is an increasing sense of stability and optimism. You feel that you are on the right track and that you will not find any circumstances in your life that you cannot handle.

With this sense of optimism and confidence, your life becomes a constant unfolding of interest and challenge.

the mandala

A mandala is a symbolic diagram, either imagined or depicted, and circular in form, often enclosing a square. In Sanskrit, *mandala* means both circle and center. It represents the unity of the outer world (the circle) and the world of the mind (the center). The seeming outer chaos of the circumference and the inner center, the "still point of the turning world," find an essential oneness in the mandala. Mandalas are a way to focus the mind, and can be found in cultures the world over as an aid to contemplation and concentration. They encourage the mind to move from the confused world of appearances into the heart of the mandala, the home of the residing deity.

In the Hindu tradition, mandalas, or *yantras*—geometric representations of deities—are believed to be alive with the spirit of the deity and are given life in ceremony. They are then used as a focus for meditation, the devotee seeking to understand and become one with the deity's wisdom and enlightenment.

Tibetan Buddhists use *thankas,* mandalas painted on silk. Each contains a wealth of symbols and meaning. At the outer rim are obstacles, such as a ring of flames or terrifying charnel grounds, to be crossed before entry to the inner palace. After these barriers, the guardians of the four gates must be faced before the seeker enters the palace to approach the enlightened mind of the Buddha within.

summer

opening

Summer is a time for happiness and rejoicing. Colorful flowers open in the warmth of the sun and there is a sense of relaxation and ease.

In meditation, the simple act of opening up, of turning toward experience, rather than backing away, begins to bring a new depth of acceptance and understanding. Gradually, we can transform our lives from being closed-in and fearful to being open and generous. The change happens spontaneously—it is like a flower with widely open petals turning toward the radiance of the sun.

month 4
month 5
month 6

month4

Normally we want to get somewhere in a hurry. Walking meditation teaches us to bring our awareness completely into the present moment.

contents:

awareness in action

The fourth month of the meditation year teaches that meditation can be found in action itself. Trying to find peace of mind does not require passivity or inaction. Genuine, lasting tranquillity ought to be steady and unwavering, and should continue even during the most turbulent of activities. Walking meditation is a practice that allows us to develop such a calmness in a very simple activity. Its many forms have always been part of spiritual and contemplative traditions the world over. There is a Latin saying that stresses its importance—*solvitur ambulando*—which translates as "you can sort it out by walking."

awareness through walking

The breathing meditation in the second month *(see pages 38-40)* used the breath as a focus. The breath is always there; it is natural and rhythmical. Like breathing, walking also has a natural rhythm, and this month offers a exercise that uses walking as a focus for developing peace, stability, and awareness.

Walking meditation can be practiced at any time. It is useful before a seated meditation as a means of becoming centered, and after meditation as a transition or bridge between the relative quietness of the breathing meditation and daily activities. If you feel sluggish and lethargic, use it instead of a seated meditation. Try the walking meditation in less formal settings, too—during a lunchtime break from work, after a hard day's work, or on holiday.

The art of a walking meditation is learning to maintain awareness as you walk, using the natural movement of each stride to cultivate mindfulness. The rhythmic and repetitive act of walking steadies the breathing, and, at the same time, steadies thought.

meditation in motion

The first exercise to learn is the formal walking meditation *(see opposite)* that, unless you are not very selfconscious, is best practiced indoors or in your backyard. Finding somewhere quiet and secluded outdoors in the natural landscape is a wonderful opportunity for practicing the meditation exercise, but be cautious: Not everyone will understand what you are doing. (A friend tried this in a quiet field and was chased by a herd of curious and increasingly energetic young bulls.)

benefits of this month's meditation

• Physical well-being
• Precision
• Relating to one step at a time
• Increased ability to enjoy the process rather than projecting the results

meditation 4— formal walking

Select a quiet place, indoors or out, in which you can walk comfortably for at least 10–20 paces in a row. Walking around and around a small room is not the best way to practice walking meditation. Work with bare feet for optimum benefit.

❶ Position yourself at one end of your walking path. Find a standing posture that feels stable and balanced. Sense the space around you, in front of you, above, and behind. Feel your feet planted firmly on the ground, and the energy rising up from the ground to the top of your head.

❷ Place the hands into *shashu* position (traditional in some forms of walking meditation) if you prefer, to increase the sense of centeredness. Make the left hand into a fist, enclosing the thumb. Cover the left fist with the right hand and hold both hands just above the navel.

meditation 4— formal walking

❸ Direct your attention to your feet. Feel the soles on the ground and the texture of the earth or floor beneath them.

❹ Begin to walk slowly. Keep your pace dignified and relaxed, but not solemn or pious. Bring your attention back to your body.

❺ With each step, be aware of the sensation of lifting the leg and placing the foot on the ground. Feel the contact with the ground on your heel, sole, then toes. Sense the shift of balance as you move from one foot to the other.

❻ Consciously relax your body and your mind. Let the motion of walking be easy and natural.

❼ As with the breathing meditation *(see pages 41-43)*, you will notice that your thoughts have been wandering. If the thoughts were fleeting and momentary, simply return gently to the motion of walking. If, however, you've been involved in a large-scale soap opera, acknowledge your thoughts by saying "thinking," or "wandering."

❽ Come back to walking with gentleness. You need not punish yourself for having wandered away. Simply acknowledge that you have been thinking, then come back to the immediacy of the present moment.

❾ Practice for 5 minutes at first, building up to 15 minutes—many people are surprised at how much concentration is necessary. After some practice, use the walking meditation to collect yourself during daily activities and to live more wakefully in the body.

informal walking meditation

When we are too centered on our own internal dramas, too full of our own subconscious gossip, we become out of touch with the world around us. Rediscover a sense of awareness by going for a walk. The act of walking literally establishes contact with the ground, and the constant input of new images helps break up fixed moods, let in fresh air, and diverts attention from a fixation on problems.

This informal walking meditation does not require any particular technique of the body or hands and so can be performed anywhere—in a city street or a park, for example. It simply focuses on maintaining awareness.

❶ Select a place in which you feel relatively secure. An unsafe part of town is not the right scene for a walking meditation.

❷ First focus yourself, bringing your mind back to your clear intention to remain aware. The purpose of the exercise is to be fully present while you take your walk.

❸ As you set off, feel the energy rising up from the ground to the top of your head. Consciously relax your body and mind. Let the motion of walking be easy and natural.

❹ Let go of mental chatter, and focus attention on the sights, sounds, smells, and sensations of the environment around you as you walk.

❺ When you notice that you have been thinking, come back to the sights and sounds around you. Simply acknowledge that you have been thinking, and return to the immediacy of the present moment.

"In walking, just walk. In sitting, just sit. Above all, don't wobble."

Yun-men

questions and answers

question

I don't seem to be getting anywhere with the walking meditation. It all seems a bit pointless. When I started I felt very enthusiastic, but I can't see any result. What should I do?

answer

Learning any new skill takes time. If you were learning to play the piano, you would not expect to be able to play well after two or three sessions. When studying a foreign language, you don't expect immediate results, but undergo a gentle process of repeating things again and again. Meditation is the same gradual process. It is also possible that your very desire for immediate results may, paradoxi-cally, be preventing you from seeing the benefits. The progress you make is always little by little. It is like going out for a walk on a foggy day. You don't notice that you are getting wet, it happens so gradually. Often you will be the last person to notice that you have changed, but one day you suddenly notice that you don't seem so anxious and tight, or that your life seems to have opened out much more and you don't seem to have so many problems.

question

Since I started to meditate, I feel as if I'm getting more neurotic than I was before. What is going wrong?

answer

Absolutely nothing is going wrong. When we start to meditate we want to experience results as quickly as possible. We hear that meditation will make us calm and centered, and we wish to experience that immediately. Somehow we expect meditation to be a pill that gives immediate results. I think what is happening is that you're noticing a lot more about yourself now that you meditate.

When you want to make changes in life, motivation often derives from feelings of low self-esteem or even active dislike for yourself. Meditation is about opening up to who you really are. It's about making friends with yourself, and that takes patience. The first step in learning to like yourself more is being able to accept all the things you might not like. Seeing clearly is the first and most important step. At first it might feel uncomfortable—the clarity is unfamiliar because normally we don't want to accept or see what is there. Seeing yourself clearly is one of the greatest benefits of meditation, but often we don't recognize it as such.

daily meditation reminders

The lessons you learn from the formal practice of walking meditation carry over into daily life. Use these brief reminders while you are walking from the subway, down a long corridor at work, or just in your own house or garden.

1 Slow down your walking and relax the body.

2 Enjoy the process of walking, rather than the goal of getting there.

3 Focus your attention out—don't get lost in thoughts.

4 Choose a place on your walk that has a distinctive feature—use it as a reminder to become aware of walking.

thoughts for the month

The path up the mountain always begins with the next step. Often, challenging enterprises are frightening, and it's hard to imagine accomplishing them—climbing to the top of the mountain seems just too hard. The walking meditation teaches how to relate to the steps themselves. When you focus on the next step rather than wholly on the goal, life becomes simpler. Huge goals seem insurmountable; small steps are easy to accomplish.

One of the most valuable lessons to be learned from walking meditation is patience: Slowing down the pace and literally feeling the ground beneath your feet allows you to shift the regular fixation on getting somewhere in a hurry. During walking meditation, you are no longer obsessed about where you are going and what to expect on arrival. The purpose of the meditation is to open up to the walking experience itself rather than what can be achieved from it, and when the goal is no longer important, the details of what is happening in the present moment come into focus. Walking meditation brings the mind back from projecting into the future, allowing you to walk precisely, with your awareness completely focused in nowness.

If you want to know the way up the mountain, ask the person who has been to the top.

the labyrinth

The rhythm of walking naturally stills the mind, and the practice of walking meditation has been an essential part of many contemplative traditions. The cloisters of cathedrals were used for a form of walking meditation; circumambulating holy mountains has been a common feature of worship among followers of the Hindu and Buddhist religions; and walking the medicine wheel has been an important ritual for Native American tribes, such as the Hopi. Some church labyrinths were designed as pilgrimages for people who were unable to undertake journeys to distant holy places. Chartres cathedral, in Paris, France, features a complex labyrinth, known as the Pilgrim's Labyrinth, carved on the floor of the nave in black stone. The six-petaled flower in the center is echoed above in the magnificent Rose Window.

In many parts of the world, places were set aside for a kind of walking meditation, and some took the form of the labyrinth or maze. Mazes in Britain were traditionally known as Troy Towns, and they follow the same form as the original ancient design of the labyrinth found in Crete.

There are two types of labyrinth. The first takes a single route straight to the center and back out again, with no choice

over direction. The second kind of labyrinth is designed to confuse and puzzle the mind with all manner of strange twists and turns and paths leading nowhere. Several paths intersect, giving many options on which way to go, ensuring that the person walking through the maze becomes lost, disorientated, and bewildered.

The essential symbolism of the labyrinth or maze is the journey to the center, and the trials and rites of passage involved in reaching that center. The labyrinth is a metaphor for the spiritual search, urging the walker to find a path through confusion and ignorance. As each moment presents new choices that lead either away from or toward the center, the labyrinth teaches that walking the path is not straightforward, but essentially about enjoying the here and now of every moment, and all life's twists and turns.

month5

When we honor the body, we experience a healing
of our emotions, our senses, and our instincts.

contents:

relaxation meditation

For many of us, stress and anxiety have become so much a part of daily life that we no longer notice their consequences. The adverse effects build up very gradually over weeks and months until they manifest in ill health. It is important to acknowledge stress before such illnesses begin to occur. Starting to honor and respect the physical body with disciplines such as meditation is one way to do this, and it can change our whole relationship with life. Too often, the dissatisfaction we feel with the body makes us inflict regimes on ourselves that do not respect the wounds and hurt accumulated over the years. Honoring the body with loving attention allows us to notice feelings and senses, and develop a larger picture of life.

All forms of meditation help physical pain and stress reveal themselves. When we slow down and sit quietly, we start to inhabit the body properly. As we do so, we begin to feel more clearly where tension has accumulated: Knotted muscles in the shoulders, tightness in the jaw, and tension in the stomach muscles all become painfully apparent.

Often we ignore the needs of the body because we believe that spirituality is only concerned with the mind. Relaxation meditation directs a kind, loving attention to every part of the body, and can bring deep healing to mind, body, and spirit.

unwinding tension

It is a common myth that relaxation is the main goal of meditation. Relaxation, however, is just one of many ways to work with the body and mind. In meditation, we seek to find the middle way between being too loose and too tight. Sometimes when meditating, particularly when using techniques that require attention or concentration, we unconsciously tense up and become too tight. Relaxation meditation is the perfect way to unwind those tight muscles and loosen up. This meditation is the only technique best performed lying down, and is useful if you have difficulty in falling asleep. Once you are familiar with the steps, however, you will find it beneficial to use in any position and throughout the day, whenever you feel tension in the body.

benefits of this month's meditation

- Reduced stress
- General relaxation
- Lowered blood pressure
- Decreased muscle tension
- Less psychosomatic illness

"It is essential that the mind and the body become motionless."

Hsier Tao-Kuang

meditation 5—relaxation

In order to know how relaxation feels, you must initially experience tension by tensing all of the muscles of the body, one by one, and keeping them tense. On days when you feel tense, practice this exercise briefly before attempting other meditations. Once familiar with the steps, you will find you can relax at will without tensing.

❶ Lie comfortably on your back. Loosen any tight clothing. Do not cross your legs or arms.

❷ Start tensing all of your muscles at your toes. Don't clench the muscles till they cramp, just tense them lightly. Tense the toes in your right foot. Then tense the toes in your left foot. Tense your right foot and your left foot, your right ankle, then your left ankle. Keep all of the muscles tense.

❸ Continue tensing the whole body part by part, working up from the feet to the neck and face. Tighten the jaw muscles. From time to time, remind yourself to tense any muscles that have loosened.

❹ Now tense your scalp and feel the tension in every part of your body. Again, tense muscles that have gone slack.

❺ Take a deep breath. Inhale and pause. Exhale and pause. Continue until the breath has relaxed your whole body.

❻ If you find it useful, verbalize the relaxation by saying to yourself, "I am completely and totally relaxed. My fingers are relaxed. My toes are relaxed. My hands are relaxed, and my feet are relaxed. My wrists are relaxed, and my ankles are relaxed." Continue throughout the body.

❼ Again verbalize the relaxation by saying to yourself, "I am completely and totally relaxed. Completely and totally peaceful. My body is light. I am melting into the earth."

Remain in this state of relaxation for 10 minutes. If any worries or anxieties disturb you, imagine them draining from your body like water. Try not to drift into sleep—you are training your mind to remain relaxed, but alert.

questions and answers

question
I love doing the relaxation exercise—I feel so calm and rested afterward–but I don't feel like practicing other forms of meditation that require more exertion. Should I just stick to the relaxation?

answer
It's good that you find the relaxation helpful. Relaxation undoubtedly leaves a feeling of well-being, but it does not necessarily tackle underlying issues in the mind. Meditation trains the mind in many ways, developing qualities such as stability, flexibility, openness, clarity, warmth, and spaciousness by using a certain amount of exertion. By all means continue with the relaxation. To bring about deep-rooted change, however, it would be better to combine relaxation with other forms of meditation.

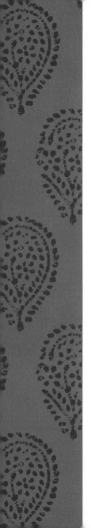

question

While I am practicing the relaxation meditation, I feel as if I am able to let go of tension, but as soon as I get up, it all comes back again very quickly. Is there any point in performing this meditation if the relaxation is so temporary?

answer

That you can experience even a temporary release of tension is good—don't be discouraged. Each time you practice the relaxation meditation, you will be starting from a slightly lower plateau of tension. You may find it useful to keep coming back to the brief relaxation reminder *(see page 100)* throughout the day. You won't be able to let go of a lifetime's accumulated tension overnight, but persevere with the relaxation meditation and you will feel the benefits.

"Flow with whatever may happen and let your mind be free: Stay centered by accepting whatever you are doing. This is the ultimate."

Chuang Tzu

daily meditation reminders

This series of relaxation steps can be performed almost anywhere, at any time. Do not practice for more than a couple of minutes each time. Don't force the relaxation—just let it happen.

1 Inhale through your mouth and partly fill your lungs, then breathe in through your nose, filling the top of the lungs. Breathe out slowly. Feel the tension flowing out.

2 Deliberately tighten the muscles you want to relax. Feel the tension. Now let the tension go and allow the muscles to become loose and soft. Feel relaxation flow into them.

3 Briefly rest your attention on every muscle in your body, from the tip of your toes to the crown of your head. When you feel a tense, tight muscle, let it loosen and relax, and, at the same time, breathe out as if sighing.

4 Turn your attention to the sensations in your shoulders, neck, and arms. Imagine warmth spreading through them, and let them become heavy and relaxed.

thoughts for the month

Men and women today are more and more concerned with keeping the body fit. We join gyms to work out, we go jogging, we try to keep slim, but often these regimes are inflicted on the body in an aggressive way because we don't like the way we look.

Conversely, the relaxation meditation works with the body in a kind and loving way. As we meditate, we notice the pain held in the body and acknowledge the feelings, memories, and images that accompany the tension and hurt. In paying attention to the stress and pain, we learn to let go. For genuine healing to take place, first we must allow ourselves to be aware of our pain.

chakras

Western science views the body primarily in terms of its physical structure, such as the different body systems, organs, and bones. Many Eastern and Western traditions, however, acknowledge that the body also has a spiritual dimension, body and mind existing on both gross and subtle levels. Ayurvedic medicine teaches that just as the physical body is pervaded by the nervous system, the subtle body has thousands of channels, *nadi*, through which flow the energy winds, *prana*. The central channel, *avadhuti*, runs from the crown of the head to the base of the spine, and along it occur several focal points known as *chakras*, energy wheels. All of the great contemplative traditions have descriptions of the subtle body and the opening of the chakras. Remarkably similar descriptions of the body and its subtle energy patterns are found all over the world, and they seem to have sprung up independently of one another.

Meditation on the chakras focuses attention on raising energy from the base of the spine up through the chakras. Freeing prana blocked in the lower centers thus unlocks emotional and spiritual energy. Meditation practices on the chakras are very powerful and can invoke rapid transformation. You should not try meditating on the chakras without the guidance of an experienced teacher.

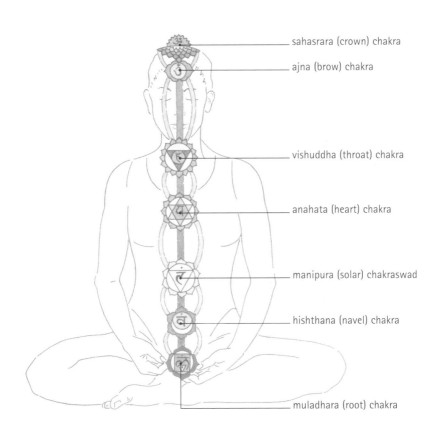

sahasrara (crown) chakra

ajna (brow) chakra

vishuddha (throat) chakra

anahata (heart) chakra

manipura (solar) chakraswad

hishthana (navel) chakra

muladhara (root) chakra

The first three chakras are based on individual qualities. The first, the "Root Support" at the base of the spine, is connected with feelings of security and attachment to the earth. As the chakra opens, it can evoke intense anxiety and apprehension, but once open, can convey unconditional trust. The second chakra, "Special Abode," centered around the genital area, opens up aspects of sexuality, and working with it may bring a release of sexual energy. The third chakra, at the solar plexus, "City of the Shining Jewel," is linked with achieving goals and power. As energy is freed here, it gives way to genuine spontaneity rather than obsessive control.

The middle chakras concern communication, and the fourth chakra, "Soundless Sound," located at the heart, is said to be the most important because it unlocks the power of compassion and love. The fifth chakra, "Purification," at the throat, is associated with expression and creativity. Working with this energy center can evoke a true sense of having found one's voice.

The last two chakras involve realization. The sixth chakra, "Command," promotes vision and understanding, and clearing it may be accompanied by a sense of profound disorientation, as old ways of seeing dissolve. Opening this chakra fully can lead to extrasensory powers of telepathy and clairvoyance. The seventh chakra, the "Thousand Petalled" Chakra of Great Bliss, is considered to be open when the energy of the individual and the cosmos dissolve into one.

kundalini

In the Hindu tradition, *kundalini* is described as the serpent energy that illuminates the whole of life when awakened. In ordinary beings, that serpent energy is said to be coiled up and sleeping. When the energy is awakened, it rises from the lowest to the highest levels, shaking off our spiritual lethargy and releasing both spiritual and physical energy. Frequent warnings have been given since ancient times about the dangers of suddenly experiencing this energy. It is said that, without a skillful teacher, the student can become like a "drunk elephant," not knowing how to direct the energy positively. When correctly released, however, the blocked energy previously used only for self-centered concerns can open the heart and allow natural compassion to radiate.

meditation in the christian tradition

All of the great religious traditions advocate different methods for finding one's own authentic nature and being true to it. There are many levels of contemplative practice, ranging from communal rituals of worship to intense, solitary meditative practice, in which the realm of thought and language is left behind.

In Western Christianity, for several centuries, the tradition of meditation was forgotten or discouraged. The great medieval monasteries put more and more emphasis on intellectual scholarship, and from about the 16th century onward, dogma became more important than spiritual practice in Western churches. This did not prevent some remarkable individuals from attaining sanctity or enlightenment, but this was a result of their intense desire to experience the love of God, and, in most cases, the individuals did not have any method to pass it on to others. Many of the great Christian mystics had a difficult relationship with the official church, and figures such as St. John of the Cross, Hildegard of Bingen, and Meister Eckhart were recognized only after great struggle.

Although there is still some suspicion of meditation from the official churches, during the last decades there has been a recovery in the tradition of Christian meditation. This has been influenced greatly by the exposure to Eastern religions and the rediscovery of the richness and profundity of the Eastern Orthodox church. A key figure in the revival of Christian meditation was the monk Dom John Main. He first learned meditation in Malaysia from a Hindu monk from the Ramakrishna Order, who taught a form of mantra meditation using a Christian word as the mantra. Later, John Main joined the Benedictine Order and discovered that the early Desert Fathers had used an almost identical meditation technique that had been lost for centuries. John Main was passionately concerned with the importance of meditation, and created many opportunities for Christians to begin serious meditative practice.

There has also been a recent upsurge of interest in the nearly forgotten traditions of Celtic spirituality. The Celtic church took on some of the colors of its pagan predecessors and retained a sense of the presence of God in the natural world. Early Celtic Christians sought out sacred places in the landscape to build their dwellings. There, in remote and inaccessible places, they devoted their lives to meditation and contemplation. Many people today are inspired by the example of the early Christian saints, and again seek out places of isolation in order to be closer to God.

There is a sea-change of understanding among the Christian community today—all over the world, people are rediscovering their lost traditions of meditation. A major consequence of meditation is a reevaluation of an earlier understanding of God. In meditation, everyone, no matter which religion they belong to, comes face to face with the universals of silence, simplicity, and stillness.

month6

Going beyond limitation—letting vastness into your mind and heart.

contents:

spaciousness

The sixth month introduces a meditation technique that encourages the development of spaciousness. Most of us often feel very unspacious, caught in a treadmill of activities and responsibilities that can seem overwhelming. We constantly rush from one activity to another, with little time for enjoyment or relaxation. Experiencing spaciousness is like suddenly finding yourself in zero gravity—able to float freely with no obstacles or restrictions. The mind, no longer tied down with small concerns, can soar into space.

Everyone has experienced such moments of freedom. The Buddha recognized that all human beings experience glimpses of enlightenment: Moments when the self-important "I" does not interfere; moments of total immediacy when the mind is not caught up in memories of the past or daydreams of the future, and is totally free. Such moments can happen at any time, and the glimpses of nowness they offer are vivid, in stark contrast to the struggles of the habitual mind. These moments of freedom cannot accurately be described, only experienced.

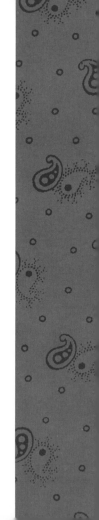

benefits of this month's meditation

- A developing awareness of spaciousness
- Greater sense of delight and spontaneity in life
- Ability to see problems from a larger perspective
- Sense of humor in dealing with difficulties
- Less psychosomatic illness
- Awareness of different points of view

letting vastness into your meditation

Experiencing spaciousness allows us to see things from different points of view, and this spacious perspective makes many concerns that seemed compelling or important lose their urgency. Other situations that previously were heavy and serious suddenly appear funny. A traditional story from Tibet illustrates this point.

"Once there was an earnest and solemn student who worked very hard with his meditation. Unfortunately, the more fervently he practiced, the more overwrought and frantic he became. Eventually, his teacher, exasperated with his student's lack of progress, devised a plan. He gave the student an instruction that he should carry a large sack of stones right to the top of a nearby mountain, without stopping for rest. The student, eager as ever to please his teacher, ran as hard as he could, with the sack getting heavier and heavier. At last he reached the top of the mountain, flung the sack to one side, and sank to the ground, exhausted. He looked out and suddenly saw a vast panorama all around him, felt the fresh air on his face, and saw clouds floating in the sky above. Without warning, things fitted into place and he suddenly understood everything his teacher had been trying so hard to teach him. He laughed when he

thought about all of the years of missing the point and struggling so hard. His earnestness and confusion melted away as he saw the vastness of the sky above and the temple below looking so insignificant."

When you perform the opening meditation on pages 114–15, you allow your mind to experience a sense of spaciousness and expansiveness. As your mind becomes more spacious, you will be able to see beyond your usual responses and experience a wider perspective.

Meditation techniques that develop spaciousness can be earned easily by most people. Before practicing this technique, however, make sure you have stabilized and centered yourself fully by working on the previous months' meditations.

meditation 6– opening

Try to find a time for this meditation when you can remain undisturbed for about 20 minutes.

❶ Sit in a comfortable, relaxed posture *(see pages 20-21)*. Focus your intention. Remember how life often leaves you feeling rushed and confused. Reflect that this meditation may help you develop spaciousness and perspective.

❷ Let your body and mind relax. You may find it useful at first to close your eyes. When you become accustomed to the technique, keep your eyes open.

❸ Center yourself by focusing on your breathing. When you feel settled, begin to recollect a time in which you felt a sense of space and vastness. Many people recall looking out of the window in a plane, sitting on a beach, watching the ocean, standing on a mountaintop, or being in the desert.

❹ Focus on the sense of vastness, of the space all around you. Visualize that sense of space, and imagine everything you see or hear is a great distance away. Feel the immenseness of the sky, and boundless space all around you.

❺ Feel that your own body has the same boundlessness as the space around you.

❻ If you feel distracted by anything, imagine that the distraction is happening a long, long way away. Come back to experiencing the vast, open space.

❼ As you breathe, let yourself dissolve into the space at the end of the out-breath.

❽ Continue to focus on the space for 10–15 minutes. If your mind gets caught up by other experiences, disengage and return to your original image of desert or ocean, etc.

❾ At the end of the meditation session, reflect briefly on your experience while you are still seated. Then gradually get up and re-orientate yourself. If you feel disoriented after the meditation, do something earthy and practical.

"Abundant clouds, a few lingering blossoms, fresh summer mountains, fragrant green leaves, and gentle cool breezes."

Rengetsu, Buddhist Nun

questions and answers

question

I feel very disorientated after this meditation. How do I know that this spaced-out feeling won't continue all the time?

answer

When you experience a deep sense of spaciousness in meditation, you may not feel, immediately afterward, as if you are back in your usual reality. This is because your mind has let go of its regular way of perceiving reality—when the mind has nothing to grasp, it has to let go. At first you might feel a little shaky after the meditation, but the feeling won't last, and soon you'll begin to feel more at ease in the spontaneity and space that this meditation brings. Balance this meditation with a more centered technique *(see pages 56–57)*; practice also the short daily reminder on page 124.

question

I seem to experience a powerful sense of opening in this meditation, but sometimes feel scared—and I'm not sure what I'm scared of. Should I stop practicing this meditation and go back to one of the previous ones?

answer

Fear is often a very good sign that the practice is working. When you experience fear in your meditation practice, it is often because your old sense of self is being eroded. Changes are taking place, and your habitual ways of thinking and old self-image don't fit any more. You may feel a sense of bewilderment at first on moving into such new territory, and spaciousness itself can be scary because it's just a little too open. Once you get accustomed to the spaciousness, you may start to enjoy the freedom and spontaneity of it.

"You will wake,
and remember,
and understand."

Robert Browning

milarepa and the demons

This traditional story from Tibet about the great yogi
Milarepa illustrates the best way to deal with fear.

"Milarepa had studied with his teacher for many years,
but the time came when he needed to meditate alone. He
found a remote cave in the high Himalayas and was
enjoying the wildness and solitude of his mountain retreat.
Austerity presented no problems to him, and he became
content with his own company. One evening, Milarepa had
a very clear and beautiful vision of his teacher. The vision
confirmed that he was doing the right thing by living in
solitude.

Immediately after the vision, Milarepa was confronted by
a band of terrifying demons who lay in wait for him outside
his cave. They shrieked and groaned at night, and during the
day hid behind rocks to jump out at him. At first, Milarepa
was terrified, and would not leave the cave. His meditation,
which had been so calm and tranquil previously, was
disturbed by a great fear that would not leave him for a
moment.

After a while, Milarepa decided that the only way to get
rid of the demons was to confront them. He plucked up the

courage to go outside and threatened them in a loud voice. Some of the smaller demons went away, leaving the most frightening ones still defiantly there. He tried many ways of expelling his terrifying visitors, but none of his methods worked.

Finally, in desperation, Milarepa realized that hostility and ill will would not succeed, and that he could not fight the demons any more. He went outside and invited them into his cave and said that he was willing to offer them his whole being. At this, the demons vanished into thin air, and Milarepa found himself alone again. Unmoved by hope and fear, he lived his life in the high mountains and became one of Tibet's most loved saints."

daily meditation reminders

This brief practice is easy and useful if you feel caught up in negative emotions such as anger, irritation, or frustration. It is also appropriate if you feel claustrophobic or speedy. As with all of the daily reminders, your intention to focus on the technique is important. Brief practice allows a moment's gap in habitual responses, and such an opening may afford you an experience quite different from your usual response—don't evaluate it too quickly, as the results are cumulative.

❶ Recall that you would like to experience spaciousness. Focus on your breathing.

❷ Breathe in. As you inhale, feel that you are breathing in space and that it is filling your whole body. Sense the space expanding in your body—feel it in your feet and toes, your arms and fingers.

❸ Breathe out. As you exhale, feel that you are breathing out space. Repeat up to three breaths. Relax your mind body.

thoughts for the month

Being confined in a small, enclosed space is claustrophobic.
Sometimes, although we feel we lack the courage to leave
that space. The habitual patterns that become painful during meditation are, at the same time, very familiar. Open
space is disquieting, but simultaneously liberating. In this
month's meditation, we learned to lean into that open,
clear space and develop the courage to leave behind the
habitual patterns of our small, limited world.

enlightenment

The word "enlightenment" literally means "to bring into the light." Light is a symbol for the power of the spirit; it illuminates darkness and spotlights and clarifies the hidden. Lighting candles is part of almost every religion's rituals, and symbolizes in a simple but profound way the transformation from darkness into light, and from ignorance into enlightenment.

More than 2,500 years ago, the Buddha sat down and, following the exertion of his search for the truth, remembered the peace and tranquillity he had known as a boy under the rose apple tree in his garden at home. He resolved to sit through the night until he understood why people caused so much suffering for themselves and others. In the morning, he perceived the world in a fresh way. He realized that people suffer because they are ignorant of the true nature of the mind. The Buddha recognized that if people could see their essential oneness with the universe, they would stop resisting change and their suffering would come to an end. He saw that everyone has the seed of enlightenment within them, and that the way to nurture that seed is through meditation. In meditation it is possible to rediscover oneness with the universe.

Enlightenment seems like a complicated concept, but it is very simple. When you understand the nature of your own mind, which is boundless and compassionate, the layers of confusion begin to thin out. It's not that you achieve enlightenment, just that slowly and gradually you become less deluded.

In the stillness and silence of meditation, that deep inner peace can be rediscovered that has been lost among the busyness and distraction of daily life. Meditation is the road to enlightenment, bringing the mind back to its true home.

fall

fruition

In the autumn you can at last relax and enjoy the results of your discipline and hard work. The rewards of meditation bring a time of release and fulfillment.

When you first begin to meditate, your main goal might be to achieve some simple peace of mind. However, as you proceed, your meditation practice deepens and begins to influence more and more areas of your life. The insight and understanding that grows surpass all that you had originally hoped for. In the fulfillment of the autumn season, that insight gradually develops into the full expression of wisdom and compassion.

month 7
month 8
month 9

month 7

Wisdom and compassion work together, like the
two wings of a bird.

contents:

contemplative meditation

The seventh month presents a contemplative meditation that helps develop a loving attitude toward others. Throughout the ages, the goal of most contemplative traditions has been the relief of humanity's suffering. The prayers and meditations of saints and spiritual leaders across the globe have included wishes for the peace, happiness, and contentment of others. Spiritual teaching is worthless if it does not show us how to develop loving kindness both toward ourselves and to other people in our lives. Wisdom and understanding have no value if we are unable to love and care for family, friends, and strangers. Even the most exalted meditational states of mind and the most exceptional spiritual accomplishments are unimportant if we cannot share our hearts with others.

Compassion is based on the willingness to respond to other people without resentment and without seeking thanks. Compassion is the active force of love: Love without attachment. When we open up to the reality of the present moment, we feel our interconnectedness with everything, and can then respond in a completely mindful way to anything that needs attention.

As a beginner to meditation, your first priority is to sort out your own problems. But then, as ego gets worn away by the practice, your own problems fade and you begin, more and more, to notice

other people and their distress. You start to feel in a very direct and natural way another person's experience. It is almost as if you were able to exchange places with that person and understand completely what he or she is going through.

Such empathy is the basis of being able to help others because it is not based on self-righteousness or pity. Thus, through meditation, the notion of actually being able to help other people begins to be a realistic possibility.

developing kindness
to yourself

Many people discover that meditation practice makes life more manageable. Emotions begin to come under control, and a degree of balance in life develops. At this point, many of us have the desire to protect our relative tranquillity by insulating ourselves from other people's chaos. However, meditation practice should not be used to establish isolation from other people. If it succeeded in doing this, it would be a self-centered, egotistical practice. Eventually, we have to open the heart and deal with the messy reality of other people and our relation ships with them.

Meditation develops two qualities that help melt hardness in the heart. The first quality is clear seeing. After some months of practice, we become very aware of everything going on in our minds. We can see our negativity accurately, feel our anger, selfishness, cowardliness, and jealousy. Because we recognize that negativity, we don't need to project these harsh feelings onto other people.

The second quality meditation heightens is trusting the goodness and softness of the heart. We learn to see that, in spite of the negativity within us, we have a tremendous capacity for feeling

and love. The combination of those two elements dissolves any feelings of self-hatred we might be harboring. This is the first step toward developing genuine compassion for others.

The practice of loving kindness that you will learn this month is aimed at developing compassion for others. The technique does not attempt to manufacture this state; rather, it allows your innate openness and love to develop naturally. The meditation is a trigger that activates the compassion you already have inside.

benefits of this month's meditation

- Making friends with yourself
- Greater capacity for empathy with other people
- Reduction of animosity toward others
- Sense of opening the heart
- Boosted capacity for love

"May all beings enjoy happiness and the root of happiness,

May they be free from suffering and the root of suffering,

May they not be separated from the great happiness

   devoid of suffering,

May they dwell in the great equanimity free from passion,

   aggression, and prejudice."

Traditional Buddhist Prayer

meditation 7—
loving kindness

The loving-kindness meditation is slightly different from the meditations you have learned and practiced in previous months. This is a contemplative practice that uses certain words, images, and phrases to cultivate a particular state of mind, and it engages all of your emotions in a new way. You deliberately use those feelings to evoke loving kindness and friendliness toward yourself and others.

❶ Sit in a relaxed but alert posture *(see pages 20-21)*.

❷ Focus your intention. Remember that during this meditation you want to get in touch with your own heart and your innate feelings of goodness.

❸ Let your mind and body relax. Let go of any thoughts that are currently preoccupying you.

➍ Recall a situation in which you felt a complete sense of well-being and contentment. Recall exactly where you were, who you were with, and precisely how you felt. Take time to reestablish that scene, and feel the sensations in your body.

➎ Find words that describe the feelings of well-being you had. You might choose words such as contentment, well-being, happiness, delight, ease—whichever feel most fitting.

➏ Let go of the details of the remembered scene . At the same time, continue to pay attention to the feelings of well-being that accompanied the scene. Remain with the sensation of well-being, and allow yourself to feel it intensely. Let the words and feelings arise together.

➐ As you experience the well-being, repeat to yourself the phrase "May I be happy," or "May I experience ease and contentment."

meditation 7— loving kindness

❽ Recall a friend or someone who has shown kindness toward you. Begin with someone for whom you feel kindness. It is better to recall a friend than a lover or family member. Keep the image of that person in your mind.

❾ Recall the feelings of well-being or happiness you generated in the first part of the meditation *(see steps 1–8)*. Let those feelings of goodness move to the area around your heart.

❿ As you are experiencing those feelings of well-being from your heart center, let them radiate to the person you were thinking about.

⓫ Recite the same phrases you repeated before, this time saying "May he/she experience ease and contentment," or "May he/she be filled with loving kindness."

⑫ When you feel some familiarity with radiating loving kindness to people you love, gradually extend the feeling to others: neighbors, family, work colleagues, animals.

⑬ Gradually extend the feeling further, to people you find difficult—those who have power over you, people who might dislike you, or those you feel negative toward.

⑭ If you are unwilling to extend the feeling of goodness in this part of the meditation, don't worry. This is natural.

⑮ When you feel that resistance, try to generate the feeling of loving kindness. If you can't generate positive feelings, don't force it; be gentle and patient with yourself.

⑯ After 5–10 minutes of working with this loving-kindness meditation, return to one of the meditation techniques from previous chapters, and continue for another 5–10 minutes.

⑰ After the meditation session, sit quietly and reflect on your experience. Having engaged all of your emotions in a new way, contemplate what you have learned.

questions and answers

question

I have tried this meditation, but it never felt real—it was always very mechanical and flat. Am I doing something wrong?

answer

It is true that, at the beginning, this practice might feel contrived. You may ask yourself "Is this real?" or "Am I just going through the motions and repeating the words?" As Westerners, we are sometimes too cynical about trusting that we do possess goodness or are capable of compassion. It's important just to press on with the meditation; eventually your mind will tire of being critical and settle down genuinely to experience loving kindness. The key is not to judge the results.

question

I really don't like doing this meditation. Instead of feeling loving kindness I feel the exact opposite, and it brings up feelings of anger and irritation. Should I stop practicing it?

answer

Try to be kind to yourself. Keep the practice very simple at first. Attempt to recall any situation in which your heart was open. Imagine yourself sitting on your mother's knee as a child, or playing with your favorite toy. Don't try to project feelings out to others if you don't feel them for yourself first. With patience, loving kindness will develop.

question

I find it fairly easy to generate loving kindness toward myself and people I love, but it gets more difficult to do this for people I hate. Is there anything I can do to help?

answer

It's important to remind yourself that what you are doing goes completely against the grain. Normally we don't wish our enemies well, so you are reversing your habitual way of thinking about the world. It is difficult, but each time you manage to generate even a small amount of good feeling toward your enemies, you are doing something very powerful. Keep encouraging yourself by bearing this in mind.

daily meditation reminders

The lessons you have learned from doing the formal
practice of the loving-kindness meditation can be useful
in daily life. Use these brief reminders in your relationships
with other people, whether they are friends, enemies,
strangers, or close family.

❶ Recall loving kindness in situations in which you see
someone in pain who you cannot realistically help.

❷ Respond to the people you meet even briefly in your
daily life with a sense of open heart.

❸ When you relate with difficult people, reflect on the
fact that they were once hurt children.

❹ Acknowledge the vulnerability beneath other people's
surface arrogance or aggression; see the wounded heart
under the thick skin.

thoughts for the month

The practice of loving kindness has far-reaching effects. It is a meditation you can work with for the rest of your life. When you embrace, rather than deny, the often painful aspects of life, you learn how to make friends with yourself. From that base develops genuine compassion for others, and, in the midst of a chaotic existence, discovery of the truth and love that are indestructible.

nowness and helping others

Nowness is elusive in meditation practice. You strive for that still point in the present moment, and it constantly slips out of your grasp. The present moment is like a flowing river; you can dip your fingers into the water but cannot grasp hold of anything.

Bringing yourself into the present moment sounds very simple, but is difficult to accomplish. We normally live life by projecting the mind forward into the future or reliving old events from the past. Living in the present moment doesn't entail excluding all thoughts of past and future, but necessitates recognizing that they should be subservient to the present moment.

The ability to be in the present moment, without past prejudices, determines how far we truly empathize with others, and the real heart of helping others is to be able to accept their feelings and emotions without running away or imposing our own prejudices. You don't need to agree with what a person is feeling. You just need to accept and acknowledge it. When people feel that another person is completely present with them, it is a powerful tool for healing.

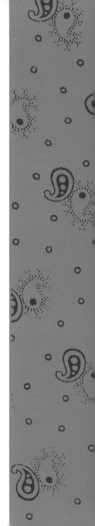

"The essence of meditation is nowness. Whatever one tries to practice, is not aimed at achieving a higher state or at following some theory or idea, but simply, without any object or ambition, trying to see what is here and now. One has to become aware of the present moment."

Chogyam Trungpa

making friends with yourself

A traditional Zen story tells of the four different kinds of horse.

"There are excellent horses, good horses, poor horses, and bad horses. The best horse always obeys the rider's commands before it even sees the whip; the second-best horse runs as well as the first one just before the whip touches it; the poor horse runs when it feels the whip on its body; and the worst horse of all runs only after the whip really hurts."

When we hear this story we all want to be the best horse; it would be strange if anyone wanted to be the worst horse. The aim of meditation practice, however, is not to be the best horse. When you meditate, it doesn't matter whether you are the best or the worst. What really matters is that you relate fully with who you are. Your imperfections may well turn out to be your finest treasure.

Usually, we are friendly only with other people or with parts of ourselves because they are pleasant or praiseworthy in some way. Making friends with yourself means making friends with every part of yourself, whether you feel it is praiseworthy or not. Instead of trying to change ourselves to fit in with how we think we should be, in meditation, we learn to accept ourselves unconditionally and allow ourselves to be human. Being human is all about making mistakes and being imperfect. What's important about making friends with yourself is that when you accept your imperfections, you no longer have the need to judge other people harshly.

Forgiving yourself for your negativity and failure makes it so much easier to forgive others for the same frailties. You no longer need to project all of those unacceptable qualities onto the people around you.

By not running away from experiences, good and bad, but seeing everything clearly, we can start all to accept ourselves in a new way, and appreciate the essential openness and sensitivity at the heart of our being.

month8

Meditation practice helps us to see the world clearly without the filter of our usual attachments and preconceptions.

contents:

delighting in the senses

Now is the time for taking delight in the pleasures of the senses. Some religious traditions have viewed sense perceptions as problematic, believing they give rise to desire, and religious communities worldwide have encouraged followers to give up worldly attachments, said to distract from the spiritual path. However, letting go of physical possessions does not wipe out psychological cravings. When we can experience the world without craving, we can appreciate things for what they are and recognize sense perceptions as sacred in themselves, as this story from India illustrates.

The prince and the yogini

Once a prince lived surrounded by utmost luxury. His chief delight, his extensive gardens, were filled with exquisite blooms. One day a *yogini*, a wandering holy woman, came to the palace. The prince, recognizing her spiritual attainment, offered food and drink, after which she preached, advising him to give up desirable things, insisting his attachment would bring unhappy karma and an unfortunate rebirth. Several times the prince refused to give up his pleasures, so finally the yogini instructed him to use his desire positively, meditating using the most beautiful flower in his garden. He did so, and after 12 years was completely enlightened.

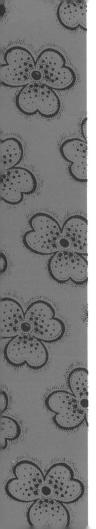

using your senses

This month's meditation alters slightly the instructions of the regular breathing meditation *(see pages 41-43)* to include the sense perceptions. Although the instructions change only a little, even small changes can make a big difference to a meditation, and this sensory meditation opens up your awareness to include your immediate environment. Many people find the change distracting, so it is best to practice for short periods only, and then return to your regular technique. However, the exercise is extremely valuable for opening your eyes to the brilliance of the everyday world.

The extended practice of this sensory meditation *(see pages 156-57)* takes the technique out into the outside world. This is a wonderful exercise that can be practiced for brief periods at any time of day and in any circumstance.

benefits of this month's meditation

- Acceptance of things as they are
- Greater awareness of your own interpretations of reality
- More accurate perceptions and centering in the present
- Sense of opening the heart
- Boosted capacity for love

meditation 8—sense perceptions

❶ Sit cross-legged or on an upright chair *(see page 20)*, back straight and upright, shoulders relaxed and open, hands on your thighs, palms facing down, mouth slightly open, eyes open, gaze down.

❷ At the beginning of the meditation, focus on the hara *(see pages 56-57)* or on your breathing until you feel relatively grounded.

❸ Relax your body and consciously soften any obvious tension or tightness. Wipe the slate and let go of thoughts.

❹ Feel the sensations of your natural breathing, relaxing into each breath. Focus your attention on the out-breath. Let the end of the out-breath go into the space of the room.

❺ When the rhythm of your breathing has settled, raise your gaze and while still paying attention to the out-breath, expand your attention into the space of the room.

❻ Allow your sense perceptions to open so that you are aware of the colors, shapes, sounds, smells, and sensations around you.

❼ When you find that you are involved in a story line, briefly ground yourself by focusing on the hara, and then return to perception of your environment.

❽ Stay focused on your environment for a short time—around five minutes—before returning to the regular breathing meditation of steps 1–4.

sense perceptions— extended practice

Sharpen your perception of the world with the second stage of the meditation that focuses on each sense in turn. There are endless fields of perception: Endless sounds, endless sights and colors, endless feelings yet to experience. You can perform this meditation almost anywhere—a city park, coffee house, museum, or beach; and while walking, sitting, or lying down. It is easier to focus, however, if the atmosphere is not too hectic.

❶ First focus yourself. The purpose of the meditation is to pay attention to your sense perceptions and to be fully present in the moment of nowness.

❷ Consciously relax your body and mind. Let go of your thoughts. Let go of the tightness and tension in your body.

❸ Open your mouth slightly to relax your jaw muscles.

❹ First, let your attention rest on the sound landscape around you. You might want to shut your eyes at first to focus more easily. Hear each sound individually—leaves, cars, planes overhead, children's voices, or the lapping of waves. Open up to each sound without any sense of judgment. Let yourself listen to harsh as well as gentler sounds.

❺ Briefly bring your attention to the hara *(see pages 56–57)* to center yourself, pay attention to your breathing, and move on to the next sense perception. Rest your attention on tactile sensation—the breeze on your face, the material of your clothes against your skin. If you are walking, touch different surfaces as you pass by—the cold of iron, the roughness of stone, the softness of grass. Again, open up to each sensation.

❻ Move through the other senses—seeing, tasting, and smelling—in the same way. Don't just appreciate beautiful things: Look for the interesting quality in everything, discovering how much is usually filtered out of perception.

questions and answers

question

With this meditation, I don't feel as though I am doing any more than sitting down and looking around. What can I do to make myself feel more focused?

answer

Watch carefully when your perception starts to turn into a story. For instance, you might be looking at the wooden floor. Before you know it, you are reminded of a wooden chair you have that is broken and are making plans to get it fixed. You are just trying to remember whether you still have the phone number of the furniture repairer, when you remember that you are meditating and come back to awareness. The purpose of this meditation is to become aware of the interpretations and stories we put onto perception. We are not particularly condemning the interpretations, merely acknowledging that they are there.

question
When I was doing the extended sensory meditation, I noticed that it was easy to be aware of the nice things but I didn't want to know about the unpleasant things. Why should I deliberately subject myself to unpleasantness?

answer
One of the purposes of this meditation is to allow you to see clearly the ways in which you manipulate your experience. When we try to reject what we don't like, we begin to close down to the world. Appreciation for perception does not mean only appreciating the beautiful things. We live in a world in which ugly things happen. Shutting down and ignoring the unpleasant aspects of life leads to confusion because you are trying to live in an unreal, ideal world. Clear seeing entails accepting things as they are. This has far-reaching consequences in life: As we stop resenting the fact that we don't have an ideal life, we begin to relate very directly with people and circumstances as they are.

daily meditation reminders

If you get caught up in painful or disturbing thoughts that can't easily be put aside, these brief reminders are helpful. They allow you to disengage from the internal monologue and locate yourself in the present moment, placing the difficult thoughts in the context of a bigger space.

❶ Breathe gently and deeply, close your eyes very briefly, then suddenly open your eyes and see.

❷ Focus your mind on the soundscape around you. Listen to each distinct sound.

❸ Relax your mind, and bring your awareness back to the sensation of sitting. Feel the areas of tension in your body and breathe warmth and softness into them.

thoughts for the month

The meditation on sense perceptions engenders a real sense of delight and interest in the environment around us. Learning to trust our perceptions connects us to this much bigger world, allowing us to see clearly that being locked into internal monologues shuts us off from the immediacy and brilliance around us. The meditation also allows us to understand how we interpret experience, filtering out what we don't want to see, hear, or touch. Seeing the nature of our interpretations allows us to appreciate the limitations we place on our world, as this story reveals.

An old woman was sitting at the door of her house on the edge of a village. A young man approached and asked, "What are the people like in this village? I am looking for a friendly place to live." The woman replied, "What were the people like in your old village?" He answered that they were unfriendly, mean, and lazy. At that, the old woman told him the people here were the same. Later, another young man came to the old woman's door, asking the same question. When asked what the people were like in his old village, he replied that they were peaceful, warm, and friendly. The old woman invited him in, saying the people in her village were like those in his old village.

"If the doors of perception
were cleansed, everything
would appear to man as it is,
infinite."

Willian Blake

making a shrine or altar

A shrine is a place to make offerings, a place to pray and meditate, a place to express gratitude or ask for help, and the custom of making a home shrine is common to many of the world's varied contemplative traditions. Having a shrine or altar focuses your intention to meditate. It is a place to come back to, a place that carries reminders of your intention to make meditation part of your daily life. Making a shrine is a wonderful way to celebrate, and every shrine should be as unique as each person. Let your background and tradition guide your particular style, but here are some useful guidelines.

❶ If possible, position the shrine in a quiet area that isn't used as a walkway.

❷ Try adopting a small tabletop, wall-hung shelf niche, or bedside table as a shrine.

❸ Give the shrine a focus in a central object, such as a picture or statue, and position other items around it.

④ Place on your shrine only objects that are meaningful to you. Other people do not need to know why you put a particular object on your shrine. The only criteria is that it speaks to you.

⑤ Use beautiful fabrics, candles, flowers, and pictures to beautify your shrine.

⑥ Change your shrine regularly. Don't let it become static. Adapt your shrine to echo the seasons and change with your inspiration.

⑦ If you have children, allow them to help decorate the shrine or, better still, make their own.

Shrines are important because they provide a setting for sacredness in the regular physical world. Many traditional cultures have always woven sacredness into every aspect of daily life, and making offerings on the family shrine is an integral part of the day's activities.

On Buddhist shrines, in front of the figure of the Buddha, bowls are placed containing offerings. These offerings are the traditional gifts that would be presented to honored guests, and they include food, drink, candles, incense, perfume, and, in symbolic form, music.

Hinduism conceives of the physical world as intertwined with the sacred, and simple wayside shrines to deities such as Kali, Ganesha, Durga, or Shiva appear beneath trees, by rivers, in fields, even on traffic islands in the middle of busy city streets. Catholic countries share a tradition of wayside shrines reminding passers by of the presence of the sacred in the everyday world.

横山廟府潘大人陳李二將軍

廟山橫

meditation in the taoist tradition

Taoism is an ancient religion that grew up in China in the very remote past. Its distant and mysterious ancestor was the legendary "Yellow Emperor," who lived around 2600 B.C.E. The text that most sums up Taoism is the Tao Te Ching, a profound and enigmatic work, believed to have been created by the fabled sage Lao Tzu.

Taoists believe that they should live in accord with the Tao, which means both "truth" and "way." They hold that, to act in accord with the Way, people should live as closely as possible to nature. Loss, decay, and death are seen as part of the same essential cycle of change as gain, growth, and life. Taoists do not try to alter these patterns of change, but aim to swim along with the currents of life like a fish in water, for when nature is taken as a guide, living became effortless, tranquil, and undisturbed. The philosophy precludes any actions that require premeditated, deliberate thought, and advocates a spontaneous and natural approach to life.

The goal of Taoist meditation is the achievement of stillness in mind and heart. In meditation, the aim is to be able to sit as motionless as a rock, closing the gates of the senses and letting the mind rest in the tranquillity of objectless awareness.

The mind should be turned in on itself to contemplate the inner radiance. The Taoist attitude to life teaches the follower to live frugally, unimpressed by wealth or fame, with no anxiety about what is going to happen and no regret for anything that has passed. For when the door is locked on the distractions of worldly life, it is easy to find stillness, and in that stillness, Taoists find the greatest joy of all—just to be.

"You ask me why I dwell
Amidst these jade green hills?
I smile. No words can tell
The stillness in my heart.
The peach-bloom on the water,
How enchantingly it drifts!
I live in another realm here
Beyond the world of men."

Li Po Tang Dynasty Poet

month9

The use of a sacred word or "mantra" protects the mind from its constant whirlpool of thoughts and brings it into one-pointed awareness.

contents:

mantra meditation

The focus of the ninth month is a form of meditation using mantra. During the last decade, the term "mantra" has entered the language of the Western world, but its context and meaning is not often understood. A mantra is a short word or phrase of varying length that is repeated over and over again during meditation. In some traditions, the mantra has no conceptual meaning; in others, the meaning of the words is important too. The word *mantra* derives from two Sanskrit words: *Manas*, "mind," gives the first syllable; the second syllable is from *trai*, meaning "protect" or "free from." Thus, *mantra* signifies both "mind protection" and "to free the mind." Using mantra in meditation helps to steady the mind while it focuses purely on the syllable or phrase, and keeps it from wandering into its usual turbulent wave of thoughts.

Traditionally, mantras were thought to have been a gift from the god Shiva. They were first seen in the Vedic period in India, and have evolved and changed since then as followers of the various contemplative traditions have experienced their power and passed on that knowledge to the next generation. Mantras are believed to have an actual physical vibration that corresponds to certain subtle vibrations within the body and in the physical universe. Because of this correspondence, the mantra acts acts upon both

body and mind. Different mantras have different effects. Some are used to generate compassion, others to produce peace, while others still are chanted to bring about an upsurge of energy. The only way truly to understand mantras is to try them out, observing and experiencing their effects personally, since the mantra's effectiveness comes not from comprehending its literal meaning, but in concentrating on the vibrations of the sound.

Over thousands of years, followers of the contemplative traditions have used these mantras and experienced their power. They have then passed on that knowledge to the next generation.

benefits of this month's meditation

- Slower breath and pulse rate
- Lowered blood pressure
- Reduced stress
- Decreased muscle tension

These benefits come from practicing the very simple mantra techniques on pages 176–79. If you choose to learn one of the more esoteric systems within a contemplative tradition, the benefits might be harder to quantify.

choosing a mantra

Most meditation practices using a mantra are taught within the great contemplative traditions. The mantras embody, in a seed form, the essence of the most profound and complex teachings. The practice of mantra recitation in the past was often given to only more advanced followers who had mastered the basic and simple meditations. Recently, however, in the West, mantra meditation has been widely taught, particularly by the Transcendental Meditation (TM) movement but also in hospitals and clinics as a powerful method of relaxing the mind.

If you follow a particular religious tradition, you will probably be most comfortable using a mantra from that belief system. Otherwise, choose a word that sounds harmonious and relaxing, and has good personal associations. Simple words such as *shalom*, "peace"; *amen*, "so be it"; or just the word *one* can be used effectively. Or you could try out the Hindu mantra *om* (pronounced ah oo mm).

shalom

peace

amen

om

so be it

meditation 9—mantra practice

Many people find reciting a mantra the most easy and relaxing way to meditate. Because of the simplicity of the technique and because the mantra is a very simple focus to return to, the practice can be performed almost anywhere.

❶ Focus your intention by reminding yourself that you would like to become more relaxed by doing the practice. Focus on the opportunity to rest your mind fully by letting the mantra fill your mind.

❷ Begin by sitting in an upright, relaxed posture *(see pages 20-21)*. You can close your eyes or keep them open.

❸ Begin the mantra meditation session either by centering yourself as described on pages 56–57, or by following the relaxation practice outlined on pages 92–93.

❹ Let your breathing become relaxed and natural. Do not attempt to change the breath to a different rhythm.

5 As you breathe out, say the mantra you have chosen. Repeat it silently and gently as you exhale.

6 Make no particular attempt to focus your attention on the in-breath.

7 Establish a rhythm with the mantra on every out-breath. Relax and let go at the end of the out-breath.

8 When you notice that you are no longer saying the mantra and are thinking about something, return gently to the focus of the mantra. When you return to the mantra, do it with an attitude of being pleased that you are coming back to awareness, rather than punishing yourself for wandering away.

9 In meditation, the important thing is to establish how often you can disengage from your thoughts and return to the focus of your meditation, in this case, the manta.

10 To finish, let the mantra go, and return to the breathing meditation on pages 41–43.

simplified mantra practice

Practice this meditation in almost any situation—while traveling on a plane or bus, out walking, or even doing simple, repetitive work. It is particularly useful when you find yourself caught up in cycles of worry and anxiety. Instead of playing over old unproductive story lines that make you tight and tense, simply return to your mantra. In such circumstances, the mantra literally cuts in to protect the mind.

Be wary, however, of using the mantra as a way of avoiding disturbing issues. It should not be a technique used to blot out thoughts and emotions that are difficult to accept. If they remain concealed, the issues will come back to haunt you.

❶ Very briefly focus on your intention to relax your mind. Look at the way your anxieties and worries cause you to tense up. Remember the harm that this tension is causing to your body and mind.

❷ Having witnessed the harm caused by your anxiety, be more willing to let go of thought gently. As you exhale, say the mantra. Repeat the mantra silently and gently each time you breathe out.

❹ When you find yourself lost in thoughts again, disengage your mind firmly but gently from the thoughts and return to the mantra.

questions and answers

question

I have been meditating now for about six months and really looked forward to doing mantra meditation. Now that I am practicing it, it doesn't seem to be what I was looking for. I have a habit of trying new things and then finding they aren't what I wanted. Should I try something else?

answer

There is no reason why you shouldn't try another technique. However, it might also be useful for you to look at your feelings of wanting. In the traditional stories, wanting is characterized as a hungry ghost that has a huge belly and a tiny pinhole mouth. The hungry ghost can never eat fast enough to satisfy his endless hunger. When we examine our own wanting, we may conclude that we will never be satisfied with anything: There is always part of us saying "If only I had this," or "If only I were better at that." What is here now is never enough. Meditation offers a way to tackle this unhelpful wanting.

question
After I have been repeating the mantra for about five minutes, it all gets muddled up and I end up saying a completely different word. What should I do?

answer
It sounds as if your awareness has slipped and you are repeating the mantra in a rather mechanical way. Perhaps it would help to use a *mala* (prayer beads). Move one of the beads each time you repeat the mantra, and see whether the movement seems to keep the words more separate. When you notice that the word is getting blurred, repeat the mantra very slowly and distinctly for a while.

daily meditation reminders

Most daily reminders are practiced very briefly in order to develop flexibility of mind. With mantra meditation, however, you can focus your attention for longer periods. Eventually, situations that cause you to feel fearful or anxious will automatically remind you to come back to using your mantra. Remember that you are not using the mantra to repress issues that need examination. The mantra should be used instead when thoughts or fears become locked into unproductive, repetitive patterns that do not reach resolution.

❶ Focus on your attention to rest your mind.

❷ At the moment you notice anxieties or worries, come back to your mantra.

❸ If you experience fear, gently repeat your mantra.

thoughts for the month

The meditative practice of mantra repetition ranges from the most simple technique to the most complex and profound rituals. In its most basic form, the mantra can be used as a means to achieve relaxation. In its most esoteric form, it has enormous power, but only for those initiated into its inner meaning. Just as a chemical formula gives power to those who know how to use it, so the mantra uncovers its power only when it is revealed by a teacher from one of the ancient traditions in which the power of creative sound is still alive.

"In the beginning was the Word, and the Word was with God, and the Word was God ... And the Word was made flesh."

Gospel of St. John

well-known hindu and buddhist mantras

If you would like to meditate using a mantra from the Hindu or Buddhist traditions, you could use one of the simple mantras below that have become well known in the West. Many of these mantras are chanted out loud and have traditional melodies (you can find many of these melodies on CD or on web sites).

• *om*—the primeval sound used at the beginning of many longer mantras in Hinduism and Buddhism. Om is the most chanted mantra in the world and is even used as a greeting between people in India.

• *govinda jaya jaya gopala jaya jaya*—I offer praise to Govinda and Gopala.

• *om namah shivaya*—Homage to Lord Shiva. Shiva is one of the three major deities of Hinduism.

- *om mani padme hum*—the Tibetan Buddhist mantra of compassion. There is a saying in Tibet that any child who could say her mother's name could also repeat this mantra.

- *om ah hum vajra guru padma siddhi hum*—the mantra of Guru Padmasambhava, who brought Buddhism to Tibet.

the heart's wisdom

Just as the fool in many contemplative traditions is believed to be closer to holiness than the learned scholar, it is the simplicity and innocence of motive that makes meditation such an important practice. A story from Tibet illustrates the point.

"One day two erudite monks were looking down from their monastery on an old man making the circuit of the sacred places, followed by a beautiful woman who they recognized as Tara, the deity of compassion. The monks asked for the man to be brought to them, and questioned him. The man amused them by his apparent stupidity: He knew nothing about Tara following him, but was just reciting the prayers as he had been taught. When he repeated the prayers, the monks recognized that the mantra he was reciting was the wrong one. They ridiculed his mistakes and taught him their correct methods. The next day, looking out of the window, the monks saw the old man again, but this time he was alone. Once more, the old man was brought to them, and, swallowing their pride, they told him to return to his familiar mantra. His simple devotion obviously had the blessing of Tara. Next day the old man was seen whispering his imperfect prayers, followed by the radiant figure of Tara."

the use of mantra in contemplative traditions

The Christian Orthodox church puts a strong emphasis on prayer. The commonly taught Jesus Prayer is used in a similar way to a mantra. The words of the prayer are simple, "Lord Jesus Christ, Son of God, have mercy on me, a sinner." This prayer, which appears to be an ordinary petitionary prayer, has been used as a meditation to bring about profound changes in consciousness. It is said aloud for a specific number of times, then constantly repeated silently, day and night. Finally, the prayer is taken down from the "head" center of consciousness, into the "heart" center, where it is said to reside, constantly repeating itself with every heartbeat.

In the Muslim tradition, repetition of the holy name of God is used as a mantra with a rosary (mala). The mala contains 99 beads that represent the Divine names; the hundredth bead is silent, signifying the name that can only be heard in Paradise.

The Muslim Sufi tradition employs a meditation (zikr) in which devotees follow a recitation like a mantra. At first, the mantra is repeated aloud, and afterward becomes silent. An ancient Sufi text states that the tongue stops reciting when the heart begins to take up the refrain.

The use of mantra began in India, and one of the greatest Indian figures of the 20th century, Mahatma Gandhi, was one of the millions who used mantras in his spiritual practice. The syllable of "Ram," a Hindu deity, was on his lips at the moment of Gandhi's assassination. Bhakti is one of the strongest schools of practice in Hinduism. One of its commonest practices is chanting the names of its deities, particularly Krishna. And chanting the Krishna mantra is no longer confined to the Indian subcontinent; the colorful Hare Krishna community has become a common feature in cities throughout the Western world. The essence of Bhakti is making the object of devotion one's central thought. Traditionally a follower of the Bhakti schools would practice repeating the mantra (japa) for many hours a day. The aim of japa is to achieve one-pointed awareness of the deity, so that the follower's individual self is absorbed into the cosmic consciousness.

In the Buddhist tradition, the use of mantras is most commonly found in Vajrayana Buddhism from Tibet. Here, mantras have been kept alive night and day on the lips of pilgrims and religious devotees in the thousands of temples throughout the country. Many other devices have been employed to keep the mantras active: Mantras have been used in prayer wheels turned by hand; in huge prayer wheels containing hundreds of mantras kept in motion by water or wind; even today on computer hard discs and CDs programmed to spin with mantras inscribed in digital form. Mantras have been inscribed from time immemorial on stones, and it was common practice to leave a mantra stone at the top of mountain passes as thanks to the gods for granting a safe journey.

winter

transformation

Winter is the time of transformation. On the surface, everything seems frozen and cold but beneath, the inner processes of change and growth are working away. In our hearts we all have the seeds of wakefulness. The practice of meditation allows these seeds to grow. We have a longing for peace and fulfillment and the practice helps us to realize these goals.

The changes in our lives happen imperceptibly and we go step by step toward understanding. After many years of gradual change, however, realization often comes suddenly, like a flash of lightning, and all sense of individuality merges into the vastness all around. There is complete unity between the universe and the self.

month 10
month 11
month 12

month 10

Being able to concentrate and focus your mind intensely gives you mental clarity and sharpness. It is like a camera lens that can bring things into crystal-clear focus.

contents:

concentration through visualization

Being able to concentrate without interruption is not easy. Usually, the mind jumps frantically and randomly from one thought to another. Examine your thoughts for just a moment and notice how quickly your mind moves from one idea to another. First you hear a sound outside, then you think of a friend who might visit, then you wonder if you have any milk, then you get up to fix the coffee. The thoughts follow one another endlessly, the mind always busy. With energy so scattered and uncontrolled, it's no wonder that it can be difficult to accomplish aims and desires. When we need to focus intensely or concentrate on something, the mind cannot settle and continues to jump in a wild fashion.

This month's core meditation *(see pages 202-203)* aims to help transform the mind's jumpiness by developing your ability to concentrate on a visualized image without interruption. Visualization is seeing with the mind's eye. Everyone can use this facility, but many people don't realize this. When you are hungry, for example, you can see exactly what you would like to appear in front of you, with no problem at all. This meditation trains the mind to use that facility and hold the image steady in a controlled way.

The second of this month's exercises *(see pages 204-205)* employs precisely the same visualization skills, but puts them to use, focusing on transmuting negative emotions. More complex forms of meditation using visualization generally require instruction from an experienced teacher. Use the meditations in this book—all of which are all safe to try—to give you a preliminary taste of each type of meditative practice, so you can decide whether to discover more about any individual forms of meditation.

Learning to concentrate has many useful benefits. As your mind becomes more focused, when faced with problems, you will be able to break down and analyze all of the issues involved. Performing the concentration meditation is like giving your mind a workout. It requires exertion, but the outcome is well worth the effort.

"Zen is not some kind of excitement, but concentration on your usual everyday routine."

Shunryu Suzuki

stabilizing your meditation

This month's meditation is not easy to do, and although it requires more exertion than some of the other techniques, it is very useful for stabilizing the mind and bringing your attention into clear focus. It is not recommended for long periods of practice each day: Do short spells on it, as you feel necessary. It is a particularly beneficial meditation when your mind feels very scattered. It is also the basis for learning to accomplish some of the more complex forms of meditation used in many of the world's contemplative traditions.

benefits of this month's meditations

- Ability to maintain a clear focus
- Development of mental stability
- Boosted concentration
- Improved memory

concentration meditation

In the traditions of India and Tibet, special diagrams, known as *yantras*, have long been used as a focus for meditation. The shapes that appear most frequently in the yantra are circles, squares, and triangles, and combining these forms produces extraordinary visual effects.

The meditation that follows requires that you select a visual focus. Start not with a complex stimulus, such as a yantra, but with a simple object, such as a pen or a wristwatch. It should be a neutral object, about which you have no strong feelings. For this meditation it is best to practice in a quiet place where you will not be disturbed.

meditation 10—concentration

❶ Sit in a relaxed but alert posture *(see pages 20-21)*.

❷ Focus your intention. This meditation focuses intently on a mental image of a physical object, such as a wristwatch.

❸ Allow the mind and body to relax. Let go of any tension in your body and mind.

❹ First look at the object you have selected. Simply observe the watch so that you can remember its features. Turn the watch around in your hand: Notice the colors, explore the shapes, and feel the different textures.

❺ Close your eyes. Relax and allow the recollection of the watch to appear. It is vital to let the image just appear in your mind's eye. Do not force yourself to see.

❻ Often you will find other images appearing in your mind. Treat them like thoughts in other practices, note their presence, disconnect from them, and then just wait for the image to appear.

❼ If, after 30 seconds or so, the image does not appear, simply open your eyes and look at the watch again for a few seconds. Then close your eyes again.

❽ Concentrate on seeing the details of the image, if any part of it appears. When the image starts to fade, open your eyes again and look carefully at the watch. It is better to keep opening your eyes over and over again to look at the object than to force the object to appear.

❾ Stay relaxed and free of expectations: Be satisfied with whatever does appear, even if it is just a blur. It's natural for the image to appear and disappear. It's also perfectly normal for the image to appear upside down. Often, you will only see a small part of the image, such as the watch hands. Don't attempt to check whether all of the details are correct. Just observe the picture in your mind's eye. Practice for a short time only.

visualization on light

This short meditation uses a very simple form of visualization. You visualize light spreading through your mind and body, neutralizing negative emotions. It is particularly effective if you are feeling heavy and despondent. You might be surprised at how effortless this form of visualization can be. Begin and end with 5–10 minutes either centering on the hara *(see pages 56–57)* or doing the basic breathing meditation *(see pages 41–43)*.

❶ Loosen tight clothing. Sit in an upright, relaxed way *(see pages 20–21)*. You may close your eyes for this meditation. Focus your intention, which is using the meditation to release any feelings of heaviness or depression.

❷ When your mind feels somewhat settled and clear, visualize above and in front of your head a sphere of white light. The light is clear, pure, translucent, and cool.

❸ Rest your attention on the light. Don't worry if the vision isn't sharp; its fine to feel its presence.

❹ Regard the light as representing all of the goodness in the world: Wisdom, clarity, compassion, love, and openness.

❺ Imagine the light decreasing in size to one inch (2.5cm) in diameter. Visualize the ball of light, concentrated and alive, descending into the top of the head and down your body.

❻ Sense the light's power particularly in your forehead, and then in your throat. Feel its clarity and whiteness. Let the light descend to your heart center, and rest awareness here.

❼ Let the light begin to diffuse and spread through your body. As it spreads, feel solid parts dissolve and become light. Sense anxieties, tension, and negativity dissolving.

❽ If you experience anything disturbing, such as noises or intense thoughts, see them, too, dissolve into the light.

❾ Gently return to your normal state. Open your eyes and bring your attention first to the body, then to your surroundings.

"In the fields, in the mountains
        I was enthralled, so enthralled;
On the way back home,
        The autumn moon accompanied me
Right to my room."

Rengetsu, Buddhist Nun

questions and answers

question

I found the first meditation very frustrating. I was trying so hard to see the image, and yet all I could see was either a dark space or completely different objects. It left me feeling very tense. What was I doing wrong?

answer

This meditation requires great patience to overcome the automatic desire for control over what appears, and when nothing happens, it can lead to frustration. It sounds as if you are trying too hard, and that effort is actually preventing the image from appearing. Relax and wait. Don't strain with your eyes to make the image appear. You should not feel you are failing if you open your eyes every few seconds to refresh your memory of the object.

question

I have really tried with this meditation for some weeks now, and I am still not able to focus on the image. Occasionally, I see a tiny flash of part of the object and then it disappears. Should I give up?

answer

Some people find the concentration meditation almost impossible, although they find other forms of meditation relatively easy. Before you give up, you could try a different, non-static form of focus. Instead of trying to visualize the wristwatch, remember a home you had as a child. In your mind's eye, walk around the house, look at the carpets, open drawers, examine the items in the kitchen. Often, people who thought they could not visualize at all find they can recall vivid and lucid scenes from the past. Everyone is capable of visualization: We do it all the time without recognizing it as such. Once you see that it is quite a simple technique, you might find the first exercise easier than you thought.

daily meditation reminders

There are many ways to use concentration and visualization exercises in everyday life. Here are a few ideas, but feel free to come up with your own, too: They are good exercises for the mind. Learning to concentrate helps you understand that your mind is something you can control rather than something that controls you.

❶ Spend a few moments consciously remembering something you did earlier. Try to remember clearly every detail.

❷ Do the concentration exercise *(see pages 202–203)* briefly during your working day with objects around you. Do not spend more than 30 seconds on the exercise.

❸ If you feel oppressed by some difficulty or problem, briefly flash your mind onto the white light above your head *(see pages 204–205)* and very quickly let that light move through your body.

❹ Spend a few moments visualizing other sensory experiences, including touch, smell, and sounds.

thoughts for the month

Concentration is a wonderful skill to develop, not particularly for its own sake, but because it provides the focus you need to accomplish more important things. Without this focus, the mind is often too scattered and diffuse to accomplish even the most simple tasks, such as remembering appointments or cooking a meal properly. And certainly, without the ability to concentrate, the mind will find any form of meditation more difficult.

balancing concentration and warmth

Being able to concentrate and focus your mind intensely gives you mental clarity and sharpness. The disadvantage of this clarity is that because the vision is so focused, it becomes easy to ignore the surrounding environment. Although the ability to concentrate and develop this clarity has great benefit for the mind, it must always be balanced by the warmth of compassion. A mind that is too brilliant and sharp needs the wider vision of love to make it whole, and a story from the Muslim Sufi tradition illustrates this point in a humorous fashion.

A fabled character called Nasruddin, whose exploits are well known throughout the world, was playing a game common in the Middle East called Remembering. It is a game that is said to have caused many family arguments, and proves how difficult it is to remember even a simple thing for any length of time. Two people make a pact to play Remembering. From then on, when either person hands anything to the other, the recipient must say "I remember." The first person in the pact to forget to say this simple phrase loses the game and has to pay a forfeit.

Nasruddin had been playing the game for several weeks with his wife. The honors were even, and they almost went crazy passing objects back and forth. But neither of them would give in, because they were both strong-willed and stubborn. Nasruddin devised a plan—he would make a trip to Mecca and bring his wife back the most extraordinary gift, so that she would forget the game.

When he returned months later, he brought the expensive gift back home, but at the front door of the house he met his wife who had a bundle in her arms. She placed the bundle gently into his arms and all thoughts of the game or of his devious plans melted away as he gazed into the radiant face of his own son.

The story of Nasruddin and his wife points in a pleasantly roundabout way to the reality of the fact that the spontaneity and warmth of love are always more important than the clarity of concentration and precision.

month 11

This month, we will be using the mind's innate ability to visualize, to deepen the experience of meditation.

contents:

upon reflection

This is the penultimate month: You have almost reached the end of your meditation year. Take the time to look back at the progress you have made in meditation, and to look forward to your plans for the future. Perhaps you are developing ideas on how to proceed, having learned which kinds of meditation feel most natural to you, and taking steps to find a path to take you further.

This month's meditation uses the lessons of last month and extends their scope, giving glimpses of the unlimited possibilities within your own mind. There is also a look at the opportunities provided by going on retreat and ways to find a meditation teacher to work with in the future.

visualization

Last month you discovered how to concentrate and apply the mind in a focused way by learning a simple visualization technique and using natural imagery to release feelings of heaviness or depression. This month's exercise deepens your experience through visualization.

We think in pictures all the time—you may already have noticed how often visual images crop up in different forms of meditation. The faces of friends and family, special places you love to visit, appetizing food, or sometimes just cartoon characters all crowd into the mind. And every night, the mind creates vivid stories and pictures in which we live a whole other life in dreams.

The mind's innate capacity to visualize can be used to deepen the meditation experience. This month's meditation employs an image of the deity Tara. In Eastern traditions, the idea of a deity is very different from that in Western, theistic cultures. Gods and goddesses in Hinduism and Buddhism are not considered to have a physical, external existence: They are simply expressions of the enlightened mind, archetypes of our deepest and fullest nature. As such, we can all share in that enlightened quality of mind.

When we identify with the pure energies of compassion, wisdom, and openness, we learn to let go of self-images of failure and limitation. The identification with those pure qualities causes a deep transformation in our very being. We no longer see ourselves as limited, ignorant, or foolish, but share the enlightened qualities of the deity within.

It may be a new realization that we habitually visualize ourselves as second-rate and inadequate; in visualization practice, we reverse that view. Seeing that we do possess enlightened qualities causes a deep transformation in the mind. Confused, mistaken self-perceptions are gradually abandoned as the potential for awakening expresses itself.

tara—the embodiment of compassion

Many of the world's great contemplative traditions use visualization as a potent way to bring about a transformation of consciousness. This month's meditation is a visualization practice from Tibet that is used for activating and working with the mind's natural kindness and clarity.

The focus for the meditation is the female deity Tara, in Tibetan, *Dolma*. The meaning of the word *Dolma* is "to free something," "to be free," or "the method of freeing." Tara was known as the "Savior who rescues all beings from the great ocean of suffering," and hers is the active, dynamic aspect of compassion that is always ready to reach out to other people's pain. She is considered to have been born from a teardrop in the eyes of the Great Buddha of Compassion.

To start the meditation that follows it is helpful to have a picture of Tara in front of you. You can use the image of Tara opposite, but if you can find a color illustration, that would be even better.

benefits of this month's meditation

- Improved self-image
- Overcoming mental obstacles
- Developing positive qualities
- Reversing negative habitual patterns

Remember that the transformation of deeply held habitual patterns is not something that happens quickly. The benefits of visualization practice are very gradual, even imperceptible at first.

meditation 11–tara visualization

❶ Sit in a comfortable, relaxed posture *(see pages 20-21)*. Focus your intention. Remember that you want to tune in to the energy and wisdom embodied in the figure of Tara. Reflect that her powerful energy and compassion are not separate from your own potential for the same compassionate activity.

❷ Begin with about five minutes of breathing meditation *(see pages 41-43)*. When your body is relaxed and your mind relatively still, begin to visualize the picture of Tara. At first, as you are reading the description of Tara in step 3, glance in a relaxed way at the illustration. Let the words and the visual image merge together.

❸ Visualize, in the space above and in front of you, Tara as the manifestation of absolute goodness. Her body is made of emerald green light, brilliant and translucent. She is seated on a royal lotus throne with right leg extended, signifying her readiness to go into action. Her left leg is folded beneath her, signifying command of her sexuality. Her left hand is at her heart, holding a fully open, beautiful blue lotus flower. Her right hand is at her knee, in the wish-granting gesture. Another blue lotus, its fully open form facing you, floats over her right shoulder. She wears exquisite silks and jewels, and the sky about her is blue and cloudless. Tara is youthful and beautiful, and she has the power to inspire energy and compassion within you.

❹ Concentrate on the image of Tara. Alternate between looking at the picture and shutting your eyes to visualize the image. As you visualize the image, make sure you get a feeling for the energy of Tara's unlimited, inexhaustible loving kindness.

❺ Now, as you sit, let your attention move to any problems or pain you are experiencing in life. Open your heart to Tara and request her help. Visualize white light appearing from her forehead and moving into yours, unlocking any blockages in your body.

❻ Visualize red light flowing from Tara's throat into yours, helping to dissolve and warm any coldness or hardness in your emotions.

❼ Visualize blue light flowing from Tara's heart into your heart, as it does so, calming and stilling the confusion and agitation of your mind.

❽ Let Tara move to the space above your head. Watch her dissolve into green light that descends down through the crown of your head to your heart center.

❾ Feel your mind and Tara's mind of clarity and compassion merge and melt into one. Remain in that state as long as you are able.

❿ Return to the breathing meditation in step 2. At the end of the session, return to your normal state in a very gradual way. Open your eyes and bring your attention first back to your body, then to your surroundings.

questions and answers

question

I was brought up in a Christian background and I am not sure how I feel about doing this sort of meditation. What should I do?

answer

If you enjoyed the meditation and felt good about visualization in general, it might be a good idea to find out about Christian contemplative traditions and the possibility of using your visualization skills within that belief system. It might also be a wonderful opportunity to examine your own habitual beliefs in the light of your meditation experience. Sometimes, meditation offers a unique chance to reevaluate and look freshly at things you had previously taken for granted. Meditation also often leads to a deeper understanding of the faith you were brought up in.

question

I enjoyed doing the meditation on Tara, but I didn't understand what all the symbolism is about. Why is it necessary?

answer

In daily life, we use symbols all the time, for the most trivial to the most profound purposes. Advertising is particularly good at using symbols to display products in a glamorous light. Very powerful inspiration can come from symbols because they touch a deeper part of our being than words alone. Symbols find their deepest communication when they can express the brilliance and clarity of the awakened mind. As you do the practice more, the external imagery begins to drop away and become internalized, and you tune in directly to the qualities embodied in the figure of Tara.

daily meditation reminder

There is only one daily reminder this month, and it is simple:
When you find yourself acting in a mean, ungenerous way,
flash back to the image of Tara, youthful, beautiful,
ceaselessly generous, and compassionate.

Deepening your practice of meditation may persuade
you to question whether you want to go further with your
search. For many people, a simple daily meditation
practice that adds depth to life and improves overall well-
being, is exactly what they had hoped for. Other people
feel unwilling to submit to the discipline of daily
meditation, but regard the practice as a useful resource to
fall back on in times of confusion or depression. For
another group of people, however, learning meditation
may be the beginning of an absorbing and fulfilling
exploration that will last throughout life.

"To see the world in a grain of sand
And heaven in a wild flower
Hold infinity in the palm of your hand
And eternity in an hour."

William Blake

finding the way forward—looking for a teacher

After practicing several different techniques, many people start to feel that they would like to stick with one type of meditation and deepen their experience. At this stage, it's useful to understand how to take your interest in meditation further. In most large Western cities there is a wealth of organizations and teachers from many different contemplative traditions. If you already feel you have a heart connection with a particular tradition, try to find out if there are local teachers available to give further meditation guidance.

There are no hard and fast rules on finding a good meditation teacher, but you might like to follow these simple guidelines.

❶ The first and most important guideline is that the person you go to for instruction should be qualified to give that instruction. Take care in finding out who the teacher trained with, and whether the tradition they belong to has approved their teaching qualification.

Working with the mind in meditation is not something to trust to an unqualified person.

❷ Make sure the teacher is someone you can open up to. There is no point in having the most highly evolved and qualified person as your teacher if you feel intimidated by him or her. You need to feel you are in safe hands and can be honest about your experience in meditation.

❸ The instructor you choose should inspire you by their example. They need not be perfect in any way, but you must feel they are honestly working with their own path and are not trying to conceal their own faults beneath a persuasive spiritual exterior.

"Teachers open the door, but you must enter by yourself."

Chinese Proverb

retreat

Going away on retreat is an excellent way to find balance in life. A retreat involves withdrawing for a few days to a quiet place where distractions are kept to a minimum. Ordinary holidays are not suited to such a quest, and a quiet day at home is most likely to end up occupied by some long-postponed task.

Every person has three essential parts of their being: The mind, the body, and the spirit. These three aspects of life are not always balanced, and they are often in conflict. For many people, the spiritual aspects of life gets pushed aside by the more pressing concerns of daily life, work, family life, and social networks. However, it is the spirit that liberates us from being trapped either in the endless whirlpool of our thoughts, or in constant attempts to find physical satisfaction. In lives filled with increasing stress and noise, many of us feel a longing to find time for ourselves. Many of us yearn for an opportunity to reflect on life, to get away from daily concerns, and put things into perspective—in essence to get some "breathing space."

Going on a retreat is simply a deliberate attempt to step outside ordinary life and relationships and to take time to rest and be still. Retreat offers a different experience for each individual, whether experienced alone or in a group.

A retreat is not an escape from reality. In this age of constant noise, distraction, and endless entertainment, being alone in silence can be a real challenge. Even after a few hours of stillness, an inner experience can begin to open up. For many people, this can be an unexpected pleasure, but for others, it can bring about a difficult confrontation with an inner space they did not know existed. On retreat, we meet ourselves head on. Suddenly there is no work, no television, no friends, no children, and no urgent tasks that require our attention.

At this point, many people find that they begin to question who they are and what their lives are about. Within the stillness of meditation, however, it is possible to reach a new experience of self that leads to a more loving response to life. Going on retreat is often an opportunity to recharge the batteries and win some breathing space. We re-enter daily life with fresh enthusiasm, having gained a new perspective and greater awareness of ourselves.

choosing a retreat

A private retreat may last from one day to many months, but most people find a long weekend the most suitable length of time to be away from everyday life.

Just as the amount of time spent on retreat varies, so, too, does the nature of the activities offered. For a serious, disciplined practitioner, retreat may involve up to 14 hours of meditation a day, with no other activities besides the essentials of eating, washing, and cleaning. In Tibet, there is a longstanding tradition of retreatants spending years in complete isolation with no companionship or distractions. At the other extreme, some retreats can be very relaxed, with time set aside for walks in the country, reading, good food, and some contemplative practice.

Before going away on retreat, it is a good idea to plan what kind of retreat you want. It may be best not to engage in any of your habitual occupations, as they can often expand to fill a large amount of time. You need to decide beforehand whether you want to listen to music or the radio, whether you intend to read books or the newspapers, and whether you are willing to switch off your mobile phone.

If you feel that you would benefit from some external discipline, it might be best to attend an organized retreat, on which the timetable is already laid out and all you need do is fit into the routine. Many people find this to be the best option because they are supported by the discipline of the group. Search the web for details of retreats, quiz your meditation teacher, or enquire among others in your faith community.

month 12

The year has come full circle; we reflect on what we have learned and look ahead to how we can use our meditation in daily life.

contents:

personal assessment

This is the time when we close the door on the old year and let the new year in. As time crosses the threshold, it's good to reflect on how, during the year, you have learned several meditations and now may be ready to commit yourself to making that practice an important part of life.

As you have experienced, there are many ways to meditate. They are not all variations on the same theme—some are very different from others—and there is no way of knowing whether one form is superior to another. Some people find they can work with one discipline better than others, and finding the right one for you is a matter of the heart rather than of the intellect. Each meditative discipline has its own flavor and history, but all can be used to transform life if you are prepared to practice them with loving care and attention. Be prepared, too, to be patient, for it is only through regular and steady practice that you will see any benefits—realization in meditation cannot be accomplished overnight.

arousing energy

This month's meditation works with energy. Energy, in this case, means both the life force that flows through all living beings and the identical energy that flows through the universe. In the Chinese system, it is known as *chi* (life force), and chi is described as being timeless, primeval, infinite, and all-pervading. When we are in harmony with this energy, we experience its unlimited, expansive qualities. When we are not in harmony, we feel helpless and limited.

The very first meditation of the year *(see pages 22-23)* demonstrated how to synchronize body and mind. We learned how to work with the posture and take our seat as if it were a throne in the center of the world. In the final meditation of the year, we will learn a technique that joins body and mind with the vast energy and wakefulness of the universe. It is a technique that can be performed formally, but its best application is the shortened version *(see pages 244-45)* for use in everyday life, particularly when you need to arouse energy and courage. The formal practice is done from a kneeling position. This posture embodies a state of mind that is calm and still but at the same time completely ready for action. It is the posture that the samurai warriors took up in their meditation.

benefits of this month's meditation

- Boosted energy
- Increased flexibility and less resistance to change
- Ability to adapt to different situations
- More spontaneity and fun
- Increased confidence and courage

meditation 12— raising energy

❶ Sit on your heels and rest your palms on your thighs. The posture should have an energetic feeling to it. (If you can't manage to kneel, sit on a straight-backed chair.)

❷ In the kneeling posture, pay particular emphasis to your head and shoulders, and sit as if you were riding a powerful horse.

❸ Keep your spine straight. Let the vertebrae feel as if they are stretching. Ease the shoulders back and feel a sense of softness and openness in the chest area.

❹ Let go of discursive thoughts, and feel the solidity of the earth beneath you. Feel your weight on the ground.

❺ Imagine the living energy all around you. Feel its boundless, unlimited, and expansive qualities. Experience the power and energy all around you, and understand that you, too, are part of that unlimited energy.

❻ Visualize that living energy coming toward you, and, at the same time, imagine your mind going out into that vast space surrounding you.

❼ When your mind and the energy of space meet, suddenly let go. Feel an abrupt sense of melting when the energy of body, mind, and the universal energies join. Enjoy the feeling of connection with that ocean of energy. Allow the current of energy to flow through you.

❽ As you sit, touch into the softness of your own heart. Feel your resistance and hardness melt away. Allow yourself to experience tenderness.

❾ Again let go of any thoughts and radiate out. Let that expansiveness and tenderness go out with the exhalation. Breathe out gently, and radiate space and gentleness.

❿ Rest for a while, then start to reorientate yourself to your immediate surroundings.

raising energy–
short practice

This short version of meditation 12 is particularly useful when you require courage and strength. As it takes only a few seconds, it can be practiced before any situation that makes you feel apprehensive, fearful, or just shy. In circumstances that cause us to feel inadequate or frightened, this short practice works directly with the fear. It seems to have more power when you are fearful because it transforms adrenaline directly into energy. Don't attempt the short practice before performing the formal longer meditation. You need to have already experienced that bank of energy and learned how to connect with it and let go.

❶ When you need to do this practice, first collect yourself and bring your attention into the present moment. Let go of fearful thoughts and anxiety.

❷ Very suddenly, feel the solidity of earth beneath you, and immediately after, sense the vastness of space above.

❸ Abruptly feel the energy of joining the solidity of earth with the vastness of heaven.

❹ Connect with the energy in that situation. Feel the energy in your body.

❺ Pause and radiate out. Breathe out and let go.

❻ Notice how, in a few seconds, you have exchanged a fearful and hesitant state of mind into one of confidence and daring.

questions and answers

question
Sometimes when I do the practice of arousing energy, I feel that it is completely genuine and I am really in contact with that energy. At other times, I feel as if I am just imagining it.

answer
Don't underestimate the power of "just imagining." One of the most important lessons we can learn from Eastern traditions is the power of creative imagination. With any form of meditation that uses imagination or visualization, there will be variability in how you experience the practice. On some days, your experience will be very direct and powerful; other days, you won't feel much at all. This is not too different from other activities in life. For instance, sometimes when you listen to a piece of music, you are overcome with emotion; on other occasions it doesn't affect you at all. Meditation practice is very similar, so try not to be dispirited on the days when you don't consciously feel the effects. Remember that meditation works on a subtle level, whatever your superficial reaction.

question

Sometimes when I do the raising energy meditation, it gives me a lot of energy and I feel more spontaneous, but I am afraid that I may get out of control. Is there any danger of that happening?

answer

We are all afraid of spontaneity because we don't really know what we are going to do and are frightened of making a fool of ourselves. Spontaneity is not the same as impulsiveness or being out of control. Acting in a spontaneous way means acting in accord with how things are, rather than our mind's version of how they are. When we have a direct connection with situations around us, action is much more accurate and appropriate. Trust yourself a bit more, and enjoy the freedom.

letting go

The Western culture we belong to places great value on holding onto things and showing perseverance and dedication. Phrases like "to the bitter end" and "keeping a firm grip on things" reveal the importance we give to tenacity and determination. Always maintaining the same point of view is seen as a positive trait, and many people believe that letting go sounds like giving up, submission, or losing control.

However, holding onto fixed points of view or fixed states of mind causes enormous problems, because in doing so we fail to acknowledge what is really happening. Though we may not realize it, we are actually holding onto fear. We keep many emotions in check because we feel that if we exposed them to others, we would be rejected or ridiculed.

We hang on and resist change in life, convincing ourselves that it is impossible and stating that "we are what we are" and nothing can alter this. Even when life is painful, often we feel incapable of adapting to new demands. It's easy to spend an entire life in this state of mind, unable to accept that we are capable of much more than we habitually think. Yet when we hang on to old routines and restrict ourselves to unrewarding and habitual responses, we limit ourselves to a small, rigid world.

Once we learn to let go and accept change and transformation, limitless possibilities open up. Letting go can confer strength and adaptability and present us with a clear view of everything around us. When we try to force the world to fit in with our expectations, we struggle endlessly. But when we let go and give in to change, we start to become flexible and open up to new possibilities that we may have missed in the past.

Meditation allows you to let go; the more you can do this, the more you will be able to wake up to endless possibilities. When you let go of rigid and inflexible habit patterns, you free yourself to realize your full creative potential.

finding the way forward—organizations that offer meditation

You do not need to be a religious person to practice meditation, but often the only instruction available is within a religious organization. You may be anxious that you could be persuaded to join a cult and should not be afraid to use your critical judgment when looking at the options for organizations offering meditation. Cults offer immediate acceptance to interested newcomers; they can appear very welcoming, and you might very well feel an immediate sense of warmth and love. That initial warmth can be deceptive. Here are some rough guidelines to use when trying to find out more about meditation centers or religious groups.

❶ Be somewhat cautious of a very enthusiastic and warm welcome—it's wise to ask yourself why the group is so keen to prove its friendliness. Is it genuine, or does it have an ulterior motive? Cults are initially very supportive, but can then become repressive and limiting.

❷ Are you being asked to pay lots of money, or is everything free? It is wise to look carefully at both extremes. Although most organizations are run by volunteers, they do have expenses for overheads such as rents, so it would be naive to expect to get everything for nothing. Ask who is paying the organization's expenses. If, on the other hand, you are asked for large sums of money, check what the money is used for and who benefits from it.

❸ Ask lots of questions. Try to find out if the followers of the organization remain dependent on it and whether the followers maintain good relationships with their families. You can learn a lot about the way in which your questions are answered. If they make members of the group anxious or impatient, be wary. Someone who is genuinely open and friendly will not be offended by probing questions, and a genuine group will welcome intelligence and curiosity.

❹ Don't be afraid of healthy cynicism—at the beginning of your path it can be extremely valuable. Since meditation helps you let down barriers to the world, it can make you vulnerable and open, so it is essential that any group you join is a safe and warm place in which to learn.

"It is good to have an end to
    journey toward:
but it is the journey that
    matters, in the end."

Ursula K. Le Guin

the year's close

Over the year you have learned several kinds of meditation. You will probably have found some of them very easy and others more difficult. The changes that happen in mind and body during meditation are hard to quantify, and it is possible that your friends and colleagues may have noticed changes in you that you were not aware of yourself. The benefits of meditation happen very gradually, but with steady, regular practice you can experience transformation in your life. It takes patience to cultivate the heart and mind in this way and to bring about the awakening of your true nature. Mindfulness, bravery, compassion and wisdom are not born overnight but nor are they remote and unattainable qualities. They can be awakened, and once awakened, will inspire others.

When you practice regularly, you may notice that the restlessness and agitation that previously dominated your life disappear and everything feels more simple. You are able to live in harmony with the world about you and the negative habits that ruled your life gradually lose their hold. Your life feels more full of interest and challenge and, because you are in touch with your own positive qualities, you are able to adapt to new situations in a spontaneous and relaxed way. The mindfulness that develops in meditation allows you to give all of your activities wholehearted attention. You can see clearly what is happening in the "now."

The obsession with your own problems gradually begins to fade away and you may find that you are becoming much more interested in how your life can help others. If you find that any of these things are true, you can truly say that your meditation year has been extremely well spent.

resources—web sites

Buddhist
www.buddhanet.net
www.shambhala.org

Christian
www.wccm.org

Hindu
www.yogasire.com
www.hindunet.org

Sufi
www.sufiorder.org
www.goldensufi.org

Taoist
www.alanwatts.com/taoism.html

resources—books

Chodron, Pema
When Things Fall Apart: Heart Advice for Difficult Times
Boston & London. Shambhala, 2000

Goldstein, Joseph, and Jack Kornfield. *Seeking the Heart of Wisdom*
Boston & London. Shambhala, 1987

Hanh, Thich Nhat
The Long Road Turns to Joy: A Guide to Walking Meditation
Berkeley, California: Parallax Press

Helminksi, Kabir Edmund
Living Presence: A Sufi Way to Mindfulness and the Essential Self
New York: JP Tarcher, 1992

Merton, Thomas
Contemplative Prayer
New York: Doubleday 1971

Merton, Thomas
The Way of Chuang Tzu
New York: New Directions 1965

Miller, Barbara Stoller
Yoga: The Discipline of Freedom. The Yoga Sutras Attributed to Patanjali
New York: Bantam Books, 1998

Trungpa, Chogyam
Shambala: The Sacred Path of the Warrior
Boston & London. Shambhala, 200